THE HITLER SALUTE

THE HITLER SALUTE

ON THE MEANING OF A GESTURE

Tilman Allert

TRANSLATED BY JEFFERSON CHASE

METROPOLITAN BOOKS
HENRY HOLT AND COMPANY
NEW YORK

Metropolitan Books
Henry Holt and Company, LLC
Publishers since 1866
175 Fifth Avenue
New York, New York 10010

Metropolitan Books® and ▥ *® are registered*
trademarks of Henry Holt and Company, LLC.

Copyright © 2005 by Eichborn Verlag, Frankfurt am Main
Translation copyright © 2008 by Metropolitan Books
All rights reserved.
Distributed in Canada by H. B. Fenn and Company Ltd.

Quotes from Samuel Beckett's German Diaries reproduced by kind permission of the
Estate of Samuel Beckett, c/o Rosica Colin Limited, London. Copyright © the Estate
of Samuel Beckett.

Originally published in Germany in 2005 under the title Der deutsche Gruß
by Eichborn Verlag, Frankfurt am Main.

Library of Congress Cataloging-in-Publication Data

Allert, Tilman.
   [Deutsche Gruss. English]
   The Hitler salute : on the meaning of a gesture / Tilman Allert.
      p.   cm.
   Translation of: Der deutsche Gruss.
   Includes bibliographical references and index.
   ISBN-13: 978-0-8050-8178-7
   ISBN-10: 0-8050-8178-X
   1. Salutations—Germany.   2. National socialism—Social aspects—Germany.
3. Political customs and rites—Germany.   4. Germany—History—1933–1945.
I. Title.
GT3050.5.G3A4513 2008
395.40943—dc22   2007035667

Henry Holt books are available for special promotions and
premiums. For details contact: Director, Special Markets.

First U.S. edition 2008
Designed by Meryl Sussman Levavi
Printed in the United States of America

10   9   8   7   6   5   4   3   2   1

Contents

THE HITLER SALUTE

An Entry from a Journal

IN 1937 SAMUEL BECKETT TOOK AN EXTENDED TRIP TO Germany. As he was walking through the streets of Regensburg, Bavaria, on March 3, a sign above the portal of the Dominican church caught his attention. He noted in his travel diary: "Walk away past Dominikanerkirche, that I don't look at, except to see on northern door notice Grüss Gott crossed out + replaced by Heil Hitler!!!"

This observation, part of the "flotsam" of names and dates with which Beckett filled his journal, became one of the many "straws" he collected so as to retain the chaotic and incoherent aspects of his experiences in the hope that he might one day understand them. Hostile to unifying theories of any sort—he found historical determinism particularly repellent—Beckett simply marked the importance of his observation through his use of punctuation. What he saw in Regensburg was added to the impressions he had taken away from interactions with Germans in Hamburg, Berlin, and elsewhere in his travels, where he had already noted the ubiquity of the Hitler salute. "Even bathroom attendants greet you with 'Heil Hitler.'" But this note, ending in three exclamation points, differs from the others with their neutral, phlegmatic tone. The three exclamation points mark the alienating and confounding nature of what caught the traveler's eye that day in Regensburg—the replacement of the word "God" with the name of the Führer. Ending in this way, Beckett's observation reads like a note to himself, a reminder to reflect on what he had seen.

But Beckett never returned to the topic. In April 1937, a month after his visit to Regensburg, he left Germany to take up permanent residence in France, and the astonishment he expressed at the incomprehensible subversion of language that was the Hitler greeting disappeared into the confused memories of a young man in search of an aesthetic identity and literary voice of his own. Interestingly, a few years later, Beckett would make his name through works that express the breakdown of human relations—their central theme—as a breakdown of language. The present book returns to those three exclamation points with which Beckett registered his intuitive horror at the rupture of meaning he sensed in the Nazi greeting. That, then, is the subject of this inquiry: how Germans greeted one another and what happened when their traditional ways of greetings were replaced by the Hitler salute.

CHAPTER ONE

Shaping the Beginning

IF WE WANT TO KNOW HOW A SOCIETY CREATES MUTUAL understanding among its members, publicly staged displays of collective goodwill can tell us little. It is not the candlelight vigil, but rather the small, everyday gestures—our forms of greetings and address, the seemingly inconsequential "Hello, how are you?" proffered by one person to another—that provide the most information about how people communicate, where they draw their boundaries, and what they choose to disclose or conceal.

When we greet someone, we turn our attention to that person and offer him or her access to ourselves in a particular way. Seen from this angle, a greeting is an initial and symbolic gift to the person to whom it is addressed. A gift in its most abstract form, it nevertheless imposes a predetermined series of concrete obligations on both parties—the greeter and the person being greeted. The greeting is the first step in a triadic sequence of offer, acceptance, and response. The briefest of gestures within the infinitely variable choreography of human encounters, the greeting opens a door between the greeter and the person greeted and assigns them specific social roles; it creates a mutual present for them and gives them access to each other's past and to a possible common future. Every greeting, even if rejected, reflects how the participants see themselves and their relationship.

Rules and formulas of salutation can change over time and often vary from region to region. A Shakespearean greeting like "Good morrow, sir!" would bring an incredulous smile to the lips of a twenty-first-century American, or even Briton, just as a typical Texan "Howdy" might sound odd on the streets of New York City. In Germany, regional differences in forms of greeting are every bit as marked, if not more so. *Grüß Gott*, the effacement of which from above the doorway of the Dominican church in Regensburg so shocked Samuel Beckett, or the Bavarian greeting of *Servus* would both seem out of place in Hamburg, whereas *Moin-Moin*, universal among the residents of Germany's northern coastal regions, or the laconic and somewhat fatalistic *Ei—Ei gude wie* of the Hessians would cause astonishment outside their respective territories. Greetings are always subject to concrete norms, and every greeting reflects the degree of civility, formality, or dignity a particular community confers on social exchange. But greetings also embody a universal social fact, insofar as they entail a fixed set of expectations that apply to every member of society, without exception. As José Ortega y Gasset has said, the greeting "is not itself a positive act, it is not a usage with a useful content of its own, it is the usage that symbolizes all others, it is the usage of usages."[1]

Greetings provide an initial structure for human interaction;

this is their privileged function. Together with rituals of taking leave, greetings moderate and frame our encounters. They define the rules and context for communication, and therein lies their central importance. Everyone recognizes the difference between a casual greeting among friends and a formal greeting at an official ceremony.

Greetings are often considered empty rituals that people perform unconsciously in order to get to what comes afterward—the ends to be achieved once the initial formalities have been dispensed with. But greetings are also signifying structures: they carry their own meanings, set their own preconditions, and entail to some extent their own outcomes. Greetings can be a "pure exchange" (to use Georg Simmel's term) or a means to an end, that is, communication; they allow us to reveal ourselves or to hide; they can bring people together or keep them apart. This double-sided nature of the greeting, together with the multitude of forms the greeting can take, make it a particularly interesting topic for evolutionary theory and the ethics of civilizations. The greeting is part of the natural history of social encounters, offering fascinating insights into the various ways members of the same species enter into contact with one another. One might think that greetings are too trivial to affect social institutions in any significant way, yet their importance should not be underestimated. It is next to impossible to conceive of a society that could do without formalized greetings or survive without those gestures people use to initiate contact with others.

ANY REFLECTION on behavior, manners, and interpersonal relationships within a specific society must begin with the question of how greetings are used, and not only in public spaces—in schools, in the workplace, and at official events—but also privately, among friends and family. The issue of how members of a culture greet one another automatically arises whenever we consider the question of normative integration within complex societies. "What holds a society together?" is the modern version of the venerable question of what makes social order possible. Every society invents its own rules governing how people should introduce themselves and take leave of one another. Often the sequence of who should greet whom first is preordained: people of lesser status before their superiors, the young before the old, men before women, new arrivals before those already present.

"Heil Hitler!"—"the properly German form of greeting" propagated by the Nazis and adopted by millions of ordinary Germans—was a historically unique phenomenon that, for the span of twelve years, politicized all communication within German society. From the moment the National Socialists came to power, this somewhat cryptic salutation, pronounced with the right arm extended and raised to eye level with the palm opened, dominated the culture of human exchange in Germany. "Now that the state of bickering political parties [that is, the Weimar Republic] has been defeated," wrote Nazi Interior Minister Wilhelm Frick in 1933 in an official interministerial memorandum, "the Hitler salute has become the German greeting." The linguistically elliptical Nazi salute—*heil* means not only "hail," but also "heal," "cure," "mend," "close," or "remedy"—superseded all prior forms of greeting and took over the familiar spaces of communication. A set of rules formulated for the National Socialist German Students' League describes this break with tradition: "The German greeting must become second nature to you. Discard your *Grüß Gott, Auf Wiedersehen, Guten Tag, Servus.*"

The directives go on to say, "All who wish to avoid the suspicion of consciously obstructionist behavior will use the Hitler salute."

The change encompassed not only the familiar routines by which Germans—orally or in writing—greeted and took leave of one another in administrative, commercial, and social contexts but also the new symbols and structures of state power. Germans were required, "without prompting," to raise their arms and utter a heartfelt "Heil Hitler!" every time the new German national anthem, the *Horst Wessel Lied*, was played or sung. People were also required to salute swastika flags and police or *Wehrmacht* officers, and when passing the consecrated sites of the National Socialist movement.

Giving the Hitler salute was a way of demonstrating one's loyalty to the Third Reich. The institution and dissemination of the new ritual marked a clear break with the previous order of social exchange and is one of the most striking examples of what historian Joachim Fest called the collective regression of the German people to "the bizarre pleasure of premodern rites."

Like Samuel Beckett, many foreign observers were disturbed by the rapidity with which the new greeting took hold. Of course, not all Germans rushed to embrace it; some were indifferent or recalcitrant or tried to ignore it. Still, it spread with incredible speed and seemingly unstoppable momentum. In the 1935 edition of the *Große Duden*, the pictorial dictionary of the German language, the "Forms of Greeting" entry already included—in fact begins with—a drawing of two men raising their arms in the Nazi salute. And at the 1936 Olympic Games in Berlin, a mere three years after the Nazis took power, the English and French delegations, in a show of deference to their German hosts, entered the stadium with arms outstretched.

But these purely public aspects of the German salute are

Illustrations for the "Forms of Greeting" entry in the 1935 edition of Der Große Duden.[2] *The first picture shows two men giving the Hitler salute.*

only part of the story. For in addition to reflecting the social order, greetings also reflect the individual's strategic understanding of how his behavior fits into that order—though not necessarily his personal beliefs. A German who enthusiastically gave the Nazi salute in public—be it at his job, on the street, or in the lobby of his apartment building—could still be staunchly opposed to it within the privacy of his home. Yet even more intriguing than the spread of the Hitler salute, its precursors, and its obvious political function is that so fundamental an element in human communication as the act of greeting another person could become so deformed. The phenomenon is altogether different from those innocuous linguistic deformations that nearly everyone makes from time to time, like the casual elision of the word "good" from the greeting "Good morning."

A recollection by Helga Hartmann, born in 1938 in the town of Bad Camberg, makes the difference clear:

> I was five years old, and my grandmother sent me, together with my seven-year-old cousin, to the post office to buy some stamps. The post office was located in a private house and was run by a young woman. We went in and said *Guten Morgen*. The post-office lady scowled at us and sent us back outside with the words, "Don't come back until you've learned your manners." We exchanged glances and didn't know what we had done wrong. My cousin thought that maybe we should have knocked. So we knocked and said *Guten Morgen* again. At that point, the post-office lady took us by the hand, led us back to the door, and showed us how, upon entering a public building, you were to salute the Führer. That's my memory of "Heil Hitler!" and it's stayed with me to this day.

A German sporting enthusiast recalled a similar scene from his youthful days in the Neptune Rowing Club in the southern

German city of Konstanz. "One evening in early 1935, when I showed up at the clubhouse for practice and greeted the others—as I always had—with the familiar *Salut,* an aggressive young kid came up to me and said in a loud voice, 'Don't you know that the proper German greeting is 'Heil Hitler!' I thought he was joking and looked around at my teammates, but there was only awkward silence. No one batted an eyelash. There was no mistake. The kid was serious. Without a word, I went to my locker and packed my things. I left the club and never returned."[3] These examples show the explicit enforcement that was required to institute the new greeting and the radical break with tradition that it represented. After all, the children at the post office were actually being very polite, and, as for the rowers, one would normally expect the arrival of their old friend and teammate to have meant more to them than his neglect of a new form of salutation.

WHEN TWO people greet each other, they step at the same time into a single temporality that presents them with an array of options. The person who opens the greeting sequence has the advantage of initiative but the burden of decision—do I greet this other person or not? The person being greeted has had his options limited, but he can still choose to accept, reject, or simply ignore the greeting—that is, to answer it or not. Yet rules like these do not completely determine the range of possibilities. Rules of greeting also provide a space in which people can express their personal attitudes toward the rules themselves and the social order that dictates them. In the case of the Hitler salute, one might give or respond to it with exaggerated heartiness or sincerity, or slur it into a mumbled *Heitler,* or try to avoid the obligation altogether by, say, cracking open the door to an office and calling out, "Is anyone here?"

Such deviations notwithstanding, we still need to ask how people could be induced to abandon their customary forms of greeting and address and replace them with an act that was so physically constraining and semantically odd—an act that, as Charlie Chaplin showed in his film *The Great Dictator*, looks ridiculous and grotesque once divorced from its ideological and social context. The answer is complex, touching as it does on people's individual histories, their awareness and acceptance of social conformity, the flexibility of their moral standards, the relationship between private behaviors and public visibility, and the desire to be true to oneself. All of these factors come into play in microsocial processes that, in a matter of seconds, determine the nature of the greeting exchange—whether in the workshop, the office, the store, the club, or even on the street. The greeting, under Hitler, became the expression of the individual's inner acceptance of the allegiance demanded by others.

IN ORDINARY German usage, the verb *heil* most often means "to cure" or "to save," and perhaps for this reason, many people have concluded that the Hitler salute was merely part of a general expectation of salvation (*Heilserwartung*), that it represented a compromise which Germans, caught between their moral scruples and their hopes for a better future, felt they had no choice but to accept. Our investigation takes us in a different direction. By situating the Hitler salute in the context of greetings in general—social practices that mediate human interactions—we can begin to understand it as not only a product of those dark and sinister times but as a contributor to them.

Germans' electoral approval of the National Socialist regime in 1933 and the collective abandonment of moral principles it expressed required an upheaval in the microsocial processes of everyday life, presaging on a small scale the larger horrors of National Socialism. The story of Nazi Germany begins with indifference, not with the frenzies of anti-Semitism, mass deportations, organized genocide. My thesis is that the collapse of morals that can permit such deprevations comes about neither suddenly nor by accident. Instead, it results from a loss of personal sovereignty and the ability to shape one's own existence. A fractured relationship to oneself precedes the underestimation of changes in social relations. Once those changes have taken place, charisma—Hitler's in this case—can let loose its monstrous power and, as Max Weber might have said, turn "rules, traditions and all ideas of what is holy" on their heads. In Germany, this process took place imperceptibly but in plain sight. People have a tendency to regard action (their own as well as that of others) only in terms of its immediate consequences and to attribute their experiences—including the experience of greeting and being greeted—to causes they do not control. Being blind in this way to one's own agency in social interactions leads to confusion about the basic criteria on which human relations rest, even before the indifference and the perversion of morals that are its objective result can set in and without anyone having to form or be able to articulate any corresponding conviction.

OUR UNDERSTANDING of how and why the brutal collective upheaval of National Socialism came into being has grown enormously in recent years. Nonetheless, it remains astonishing that Germans were willing to sacrifice, as historian Sebastian Haffner has said, their "reserves of pride, conviction, self-confidence, and dignity," and demonstrate their submission to Hitler even in the act of greeting. Germany was not the only nation in the early twentieth century to be caught up in an exaggerated need for connection and conformity. But what interests us is not so much the populist passions as the shifts in basic social behaviors and attitudes. The Hitler salute, National Socialism's hallmark gesture, took a normal social situation and imbued it with the threat of sanction and punishment. Where did it come from? How did it spread? To what extent did Germans conform to the mandatory greeting? In what ways did they oppose it or come to some kind of compromise with it? And what were the preconditions for its internalization and acceptance?

The life span of the Nazi salute seems fleeting when viewed against the more enduring catastrophes produced by National Socialism, yet during the twelve years in which it held sway, its ghostly spectacle invested every human encounter with magical fascination and helped to silence a nation's moral scruples. The Nazi salute thus marked Germany's regression into a state of moral disregard in two ways: it stamped out the act of communication—the very heart of the human encounter—with the sign of the failure, and it signaled the triumph of social radicalism over the fragile space of human dignity and interaction.

CHAPTER TWO

The Greeting as Initial Gift

THE NAZI PARTY PROPAGATED THE HITLER SALUTE AS THE only properly German form of greeting, and indeed Germans today still refer to it, albeit negatively, as "the German greeting." The name reflects the greeting's obligatory nature and at the same time marks an intrusion by the state into what Hegel called *Sittlichkeit* ("ethical life"), out of which, according to Hegel's *Philosophy of Right*, the state itself develops. In reality, members of a single linguistic community greet one another in a variety of ways. Germans, of course, greet one another in German, and in so doing they can be distinguished from the Dutch, the French, or the Poles. But before Nazism, there was no such thing as *the* German greeting.

In July 1933, an interministerial decree was issued that made the greeting compulsory in official state business, and a few months later the requirement was extended to include public encounters of all sorts. Germans were ordered to use "Heil Hitler" in their written correspondence and to give the salute in government offices and in the presence of Nazi flags or party members in uniform. Within a matter of weeks Germans began to see nothing out of the ordinary in certifying commercial contracts, financial statements, or payroll lists with the concluding phrase "With German Greetings, Heil Hitler" or simply "Heil Hitler."

The new greeting spread rapidly throughout the public sphere, where the visibility of communication is greatest. How many people violated the injunction and refused to salute is unknown, but we do know that from 1933 onward, those who refused to use the new greeting could be prosecuted in special courts and if convicted were fined or sent to concentration camps. In any case, it quickly became clear that the Hitler salute could be used to gauge adherence to the new regime, to check on people's loyalty to the Third Reich. Ironically, as the salutation became more and more widely used, it no longer served as a battle cry for the National Socialist movement since it didn't necessarily indicate a person's membership in the Nazi Party. The phrase "Heil Hitler!" lost its heroic pathos and was sucked into the routines of everyday life. Once it ceased being a confession of faith and became a stock phrase, it was perilously open to ambiguity. Photographs of vacationers saluting a sand sculpture of Hitler at a popular beach resort on the island of Sylt, or of jazz-loving youth around Emil Mangelsdorff and his Hot Club saluting one another with the "Swing Heil," show the new ritual's potential for parody.

Up to this point, we have been calling the Hitler salute a greeting, in keeping with the German usage, yet is that really what it was? Did the Hitler salute do what greetings normally do, that is, open up the possibility of communication? If we confine ourselves to situations in which it was used as a matter of habit, in place of traditional forms of salutation, the answer is,

Vacationers on the island of Sylt saluting a sand sculpture of Hitler's head.

Frankfurt musician Emil Mangelsdorff and friends from the Hot Club performing the "Swing Heil."

or would seem to be, obviously yes. But the picture changes if we look more closely at the ritual's component elements and bear in mind that greetings are subject to two very different kinds of rules: the general rules that apply systematically to all greetings, and the specific rules that give a greeting its particular and contingent historical form. Making this distinction can help us determine the extent to which the Hitler salute fulfilled the greeting's usual function. Let us then begin with a short conceptual sketch of the significance of greetings in general.[1]

THE FACT that the elements of the greeting—offer, acceptance, and response—occur in simple succession makes it clear that we are dealing with a sequential practice, at each stage of which various behavioral options are embedded. The options differ according to which of the two parties takes the initiative and greets first—just as, in a game of chess, much depends on which player gets to make the first move. Each stage in the sequence logically implies the one preceding it—if I respond to a greeting, I have already accepted the greeter's opening gambit—but the reverse is not true. A greeting can be accepted as a self-contained act, that is, the person being greeted need not respond and in certain cases may not even be expected to. (The seemingly superfluous stipulation that the Hitler salute was to be performed "without prompting" is one example of this sequential logic.) It is also worth noting that the first stage of the greeting, the offer, does not necessarily begin an exchange. What it does do is close whatever activity preceded it. If I say hello to someone, I necessarily stop what I was previously doing or at least bracket it for the duration of the greeting sequence.

The act of greeting is the foundation of sociality. It is through the greeting that reciprocity, which is basic to human existence, can arise. It is hardly surprising then that the two extremes of human existence—birth and death—are apprehended in terms of the metaphor of greeting. There is scarcely a form of human exchange that does not depend on the greeting as an articulation of contact, confirmation of social membership, and invitation to proceed with a future course of activity.[2] This is true as well of the "final farewell" that is said when the casket has been lowered into the grave. Even as expressions of leave-taking go, graveside farewells are particularly conclusive—no one expects the deceased to respond. With the person to whom the farewell is addressed released from normal obligations of leave-taking, a silence that in other circumstances might signal rejection or rupture here does quite the opposite: it leaves open the possibility that the bereaved might continue his relationship with the deceased, or perhaps begin a new one with him. If "in the beginning there was the Word," then it had to have been a word of greeting, for the greeting is the primordial form of human exchange.

Every greeting involves a decision—whether or not to greet. Not only is that decision a risky one but so, too, is the situation of contact in which it must be made. The etymology of the word "greet" reflects this potential danger. *Grüßen*, German for "to greet," comes from the Middle High German verb *gruozen*, which primarily meant "to bring to speech," but which could also connote challenge and even attack. The greeting is not a harmlessly hollow gesture; rather, it is a way of negotiating the crisis implicit in any potential encounter with another person. It is not the only way; convocations, threats, and dissimulation, as well as violence and dispossession, are possible alternatives, as are supplications, benedictions, tributes, congratulations, gifts, and sharing food. Gestures of submission—or, as sociologists would say, "of inequality"—such as bowing to another person or kissing his feet show just how critical an encounter can be, par-ticularly when the relationship between the participants is asymmetrical, as it so often is. The evolution of *Homo sapiens* as a species capable of walking upright, together with the liberation of the field of vision that it entailed, opened up new possibilities for establishing contact. Posture, the positioning of the head, arms, and legs, became a medium for human beings to create proximity. In Western culture, the hand became the preferred means for gestures intended to initiate human exchange. The gesture of shaking hands underscores two individuals' mutual openness and at the same time rules out the possibility of their using weapons against each other.[3]

A greeting can reinitiate a relationship that has been interrupted or create a new one altogether; one can greet an acquaintance, or greet in order to make an acquaintance. In an established relationship—between lovers, for example—the greeting communicates continuity and, with the help of kisses and embraces, reaffirms the initial promise of love—the mutual expectation of a lasting bond. When two lovers say "Good morning" to each other upon awakening in bed, they bridge the hiatus that sleeping and dreaming, which isolate them as individuals, have created in their relationship during the night. As for "Good night," it is not a leave-taking formula like any other, at least not in Germany. There, it tends to be reserved for relationships that one can count on to continue.

We do not have the space here to examine all the variations of confirming an existing relationship, so we will concentrate on areas where the greeting serves both to demarcate a boundary between the actors and to move them beyond it into a space of mutual accessibility. In this regard the greeting is the communicative procedure by which human beings emerge from the primitive safety of egocentricity and enter the public sphere. It is the first communicative act that crosses the threshold of private activity, serving, as German ethnographer Arnold van Gennep would say, as a "rite of passage" toward the different types of sociality in which human life is realized.[4]

If the greeting seems to be a routine form of communication, it is so only from the perspective of the participants. From the theoretical and historical perspective, the greeting is, as we have said, a response to the crisis that is the human encounter. In the highly dramatic uncertainty that lies at the heart of the greeting we find two possibilities: either we regard the Other as an object, who interests us to the extent that we perceive him as attractive or dangerous, or we can see the Other as a partner in a possible collaboration—someone who interests us not because of what we could do *to* him but because of what we might be able to do *with* him. The greeting, or the lack thereof, reveals which of these two options—aggression or cooperation— the initiator has chosen. Attacks or raids are not preceded by greetings, for they invalidate the minimum of interpersonal symmetry that it is the role of the greeting to express and instead seek to maximize the advantage of one side.

Not surprisingly, then, three norms appear again and again as the "raw material" of greetings: *physical integrity or health*— our own, which we announce, or that of the other person, which the greeting inquires after or expresses as a wish for him; a *willingness to cooperate*—here again, our own willingness, which we announce, or the other person's willingness, which the greeting helps us to assess; and, lastly, *peacefulness*, which is often inscribed in the greeting itself and which we invite the other to verify. These three norms can occur individually or in conjunction with one another, but whatever the case, the universal structure of the obligations of the greeting remains the same. That structure can be summarized as follows:

1. The act of greeting creates an obligation of reciprocity. The sequence of offering, accepting, and responding is the simplest

form of human sociality. In a situation in which people are uncertain how to behave, the greeting attempts to establish symmetry between them (or, as in the particular case of genuflection, to enable an exchange to take place despite a difference in rank or status). The greeting creates an obligation on both sides, demanding that each party recognize, respect, and, at least potentially, cooperate with the other. The act of greeting is an overture, signaling one's interest in the other person, and proposing that the two emerge from anonymity and make each other's acquaintance. At the same time, the process of greeting invokes the idea of limits and exclusion. In building a bridge to another person, the greeting designates a gulf that must be spanned, a border that must be crossed.

2. The greeting places the partners in communication in the shared spatiotemporality of the here and now, and it allows or compels them to define themselves with respect to a common future. In situating themselves within the horizon of the greeting, the participants assert their freedom of action and, at the same time, acknowledge the limits of that freedom. Every "Hello" or "Good evening" signifies that the person offering the greeting has acceded to the rule that a greeting be given. The greeter presents himself to the other as an individual who has chosen to follow this rule rather than neglecting or disregarding it. In this way, the individual asserts his autonomy with respect to the rule. This holds true both for the greeter and the person being greeted and applies, moreover, to all human actions: when it comes to following rules, people conform more or less, and it is precisely through this "more or less" that they express their individuality.

3. The greeting creates or brings closure to a potential relationship. A relationship that has been commenced by a
greeting can of course be interrupted in the moment of expected return—for example, if the intended recipient slams
a door in the greeter's face or turns away without saying a
word. Even then, the rupture is understood as relating back
to the greeting and is judged within that context. Greetings
and good-byes form a single unit within which there are different gradations corresponding to the different meanings
of the word "present." German sociologist Ulrich Oevermann defines those meanings as "'present' as in temporal
presence, indicating simultaneity with an event that is
within my field of awareness; 'present' as in spatial presence in the sense that we speak of someone as being present at something; and 'present' as in the sense of a symbolic
expression of my unconditional acknowledgment of another person in the form of a gift—and with it my ideal
presence with that other person."[5] The southern German
custom of greeting others at the marketplace with the elliptical *Au do?* ("You too?") invokes mutual presence in both
the spatial and temporal sense, alerting the other to the fact
that the greeter is also at the market and, in the time it takes
to await the response, testing the other's willingness to communicate.

Human beings and animals diverge most from one another
in their perception of time, and the divergence is particularly evident in the rituals of bidding good-bye. Animals, unable to imag-
ine a future and thus the possibility of reunion, do not perform
them. Ethnographer Raymond Firth writes: "The ability of an an-
imal to differentiate the *length of time* during which another is

absent seems fairly limited. Human parting conceptualizes a future with a time scale and the ritual is modified accordingly."[6]

Every greeting joins together two analytically distinguishable generative principles: an offer of reciprocity, which is of universal value, and the historically specific social norms that regulate that offer. This duality applies both to what is said in the greeting as well as to the gestures that accompany the verbal message, either to confirm or emphasize it. Historically, the nonverbal components of the greeting—eyes, tone of voice, spatial disposition of the body—express a willingness to submit to the other or a readiness to defend oneself against him, whereas the linguistic components express the idea of symmetry. Through the interplay of these various elements, the act of greeting can be refined and particularized. Yet above and beyond the sociological and historical principles that give it its concrete form, the greeting has a moral dimension: in the act of greeting, people acknowledge that their connection to and dependence on others is a sign of their own moral character. It is for this reason that in all religions, the greeting—think of the greetings of peace in the liturgies of the three major monotheistic religions—has so privileged a status.

CHAPTER THREE

German Greetings

To GRASP THE SIGNIFICANCE OF THE "HEIL HITLER" RIT-
ual, we need to consider the broader universe of German greetings. Greeting conventions are part of every community's cultural
heritage, and like any social good, they develop over time. They
are often regional, and their use tends to be restricted to particular generations or occupations, social microcosms whose members reaffirm their common bond and shared affiliation by
greeting one another in specific and formulaic ways. The greeting *Glück auf* ("Best of luck"), for instance, used among coal
miners in the Ruhr Valley region of western Germany, speaks to
the perilous nature of their occupation. In contrast, the exclusively northern German *Moin-Moin* —whose now-obscure literal
meaning derives from "good" as in "Good morning" or "Good
evening"—communicates regional rather than class allegiance.
Yet in both cases, the greeting serves to indicate membership in a
community that, by choice or by tradition, has set itself apart
from the surrounding society and its conventions.

Some forms of address, however, like the neutral *Guten Tag,* transcend the confines of localized meanings. Used in conjunction with the addressee's title—as in *Guten Tag, Herr Direktor* or *Guten Tag, Herr Professor*—they signal social status, but they can also be used alone, thus allowing people to avoid invoking position and rank. The greetings in wide use in Germany in the early years of the twentieth century show considerable variations. But if there was no one standard or even predominant German greeting, there was the desire for one—an expression perhaps of a general wish for national unity in reaction to Germany's territorial history as a mosaic of small feudal states in which people tended to identify with their

A postcard from around 1900 shows how the desire for national unity was expressed in the desire for unified standards of greeting. It reads, "The only acceptable German greetings are 'Greet God,' 'Good morning,' 'Good day,' 'Good evening,' 'Good night,' 'Farewell,' and 'Until we meet again.'"

region, ethicity, or occupation. In contrast to what happened in France, German greeting conventions were never entirely subsumed under a single standard practice, and many of the linguistic formulas and accompanying physical gestures are the result of a highly nuanced social order.

A number of expressions still in use bear the imprint of the courtly conventions of feudal society. *Küss' die Hand* ("Kiss your hand") or *Gestatten Sie* ("With your permission") reflect, in the humility of their formulations, social conventions of a pre-bourgeois society, conventions that later became "class symmetrical" under the influence of the idea of Christian equality in the eyes of God. Reference to social status in the greeting is a relic of modes of interaction from a time when the greeting had to communicate the initiator's unquestioning acceptance of the other person's status, thereby assuring the person receiving the greeting that he would receive his due. At their most extreme, such greetings could take the form of exaggerated demonstrations of subservience and empty court ritual. The typically southern German *Servus* reflects the tendency of greetings to evolve into symmetrical forms. Literally, it means "I serve you," but in current usage, the person greeted in this way responds in kind, thus establishing equality in rank.

As a rule, the literal meaning of today's greetings are obscure, and their significance as social acts can be difficult to decipher. Rarely is it possible to identify a single original context. In the Occidental world, greetings are, almost without exception, influenced by the Christian ideal of individual moral equality before the Creator. Greetings that express this ideal are well-suited to the forms of labor characteristic of the modern age, which require more frequent and intense contact between people, as well as greater mobility. Under these circumstances, individuals are encouraged to abandon locally specific greeting traditions and seek formulations that can be adapted flexibly to fit a variety of situations.

In German, the most common example of a modern, flexible greeting is *Guten Tag* ("Good day") together with the variants *Guten Morgen* ("Good morning") and *Guten Abend* ("Good evening"). Used most often in business or official situations between people who are not very well acquainted, all three of these formulations limit the scope of the initiated interaction with an explicit reference to time. On the surface, the greeting *Guten Tag* merely expresses a wish that the recipient have a good day, although there is an undercurrent that suggests that the greeter will do what he or she can to help realize that wish. It also implies that the typical human situation is one of activity, and it pledges, again implicitly, that the business of the person greeted will not suffer unduly from the interruption by the greeter.

The phrase *Guten Tag*, moreover, alludes to the notion that man was created in God's image, sharing with his deity the duty of daily creative practice and the subsequent evaluation of the results—"And He saw that it was good." The religious context, unstated, reflects the typically Protestant conflation of religious values and labor that sociologist Helmuth Plessner calls "worldly piety." The connection is more readily apparent in early versions of the greeting such as *Gott wünscht Dir einen guten Tag* ("God wishes you a good day") or *Möge Gott Dir einen guten Tag wünschen* ("May God wish you a good day"). These formulations refer to a specific period of time, not to social status or allegiance, and the anticipated relationship and duties entailed therein remain temporally limited. Over the course of history, the religious origins of *Guten Tag* have been eroded, allowing the greeting to attain a high degree of universality; it can be used by anyone regardless of social milieu.

Neutral from the point of view of affiliation, *Guten Tag* differs dramatically from *Grüß Gott* ("Greet God"), the common greeting in Catholic southern Germany. This latter greeting does not refer to time. Instead, it reflects a set of cultural values that bind the greeting's initiator and its recipient in a single, religiously defined group. Its historical antecedents are *Gott möge Dich grüßen* ("May God greet you")—primarily a written expression—and the medieval *Gott zum Grusse* ("For God, with greetings").

All of these greetings raise the following question: why should those who greet each other invoke a third party, when the act of greeting itself concerns only the parties present? Formulations like *Grüß Gott* expand the communicative situation to include an idealized presence that in some sense presides over the encounter. The person giving this greeting invokes an imagined authority under whose aegis the encounter is now to be situated. Two functions are thus served: on the one hand, when greeting an interlocutor who is either unknown and thus potentially hostile, or someone whose prior relationship with the greeter must be reaffirmed, the greeter seeks the assistance of a third party; on the other hand, the greeter ensures a peaceful encounter by including the other person within the moral sphere defined by a supernatural authority. A third party—in this case, God—is therefore entrusted with maintaining the symmetry of the interaction and "bringing the other to speech." In this reading, the greeting *Grüß Gott* alludes to the monotheistic belief in an omnipresent, infinite, and infinitely powerful God. In a slightly more subtle version of this reading, the initiator of the greeting implicitly casts himself as the representative or mouthpiece of the divine authority he invokes, thereby removing some of the uncertainty inherent in any meeting.

Compared with *Guten Tag*, in which the act of greeting is time-bound and morally neutral, *Grüß Gott* more clearly articulates the greeter's sense of belonging to a community whose members share the same values—Christian values—and expresses the assumption that the person being greeted is a member of that community as well. The human encounter is mediated by the idea of a community united in their fear of the Divine. The participants entrust themselves to the deity, giving Him control over this crucial initial moment in their encounter. In other words, the greeter expresses his faith in God's ability to keep the peace and assumes that the person he is greeting shares that faith. This is true regardless of the fervency with which the participants maintain their religious beliefs. No matter whether the greeting is performed out of conviction or mere habit, its social function remains basically the same.

CHAPTER FOUR

An Oath by Any Other Name

With the Hitler salute, a new variant took its place in the repertoire of German greeting conventions. On July 13, 1933—a scant six months after Hitler became German chancellor and one day before all other political parties were banned—the Reich issued an edict defining the Hitler greeting as a general civic duty and making its use mandatory in all party and state buildings and at commemorative sites. The new convention was widely and enthusiastically adopted in the first few years of the Third Reich, when the Nazi Party was still consolidating its power.

Every act of greeting someone, or refusing to do so, is an act of individual self-definition. In the case of "Heil Hitler," the laws mandating its use forced Germans to define themselves and their values in relationship to the Führer, bringing him as the unseen mediating third party into every social encounter. Seen within the historical and cultural context of previous greetings—including everything from the kissing of hands to the tipping of hats, from regionalisms like *Moin-Moin* to the bourgeois *Guten Tag*, from the curtsy of little girls to the bow at the waist expected of little boys—the "Heil Hitler" ritual promised to simplify social interactions, both professional and personal. It offered a seemingly direct and uncomplicated way to establish contact, putting an end to elaborate rules of etiquette and neutralizing the class pretensions that could darken any encounter with the shadow of social inequality. In the early years of the Third Reich, it was said the Hitler greeting had done away with subservience in all its forms.

Initially it was unclear exactly how and when the new greeting was to be used. This confusion led to a series of decrees and interministerial memoranda codifying its precise wording and accompanying gestures. One such decree from the Reich Interior Ministry on January 22, 1935, read:

> The law of August 1, 1934, concerning the head of the German Empire and the law of August 20, 1934, concerning the oaths taken by civil servants and members of the *Wehrmacht* have created a highly personal and insoluble bond of loyalty between the German civil service and the Führer and Reich chancellor. I am convinced that the civil servants and the other workers within the public administration will voluntarily and joyfully express this bond by using the German greeting. I therefore order that civil servants and other employees henceforth use the German greeting while performing their duties and in their place of employment by raising their right

> hands—or in case of physical infirmity their left ones—and clearly articulating the words "Heil Hitler." And I expect from civil servants and other public employees that they use the same form of greeting at other times as well.

Encounters in public spaces weren't the only situations to which the edict applied. Even the most routine and utilitarian communications—business letters, bank statements, order forms, delivery receipts, and the like—now had to end with a standard formula. The phrase "With German greetings," popularized in the early 1920s, when it expressed Germans' longing for a homogeneous national culture in the aftermath of Germany's defeat in World War I, was the required closing salutation in commercial communications, replacing earlier customary expressions. In official government correspondence, however, the standard written form for taking leave was "Heil Hitler."

The Hitler salute occupied a special place among the many displays of loyalty that were mandated and staged during the years of the Reich. It was different from the ritual used at mass rallies, where enthusiastic crowds answered *Heil* to the call of *Sieg* ("victory"), thus proclaiming their commitment to the glorious struggle and their belief in Germany's ultimate triumph. It also differed from the reverential rituals surrounding flag raisings or the singing of the national anthem. The Hitler salute represented the complete transformation of what until then had been universally accepted rules of greeting that spoke to the individual's sense of self and personal values.

Establishing the greeting's authenticity became the goal of

Nazi propaganda. As the main Nazi newspaper, the *Völkischer Beobachter*, wrote in 1935, "One emerging task is to commit people to the majestic German greeting. . . . When we issue the German greeting as an expression of the state of our character to those who may still have doubts, we should be watchful that it is neither falsified nor deformed. These words of greeting . . . should continually raise us from the mundane details of everyday life and remind us of the grand goal and challenges Adolf Hitler has given to us all. . . . This is a bit of practical National Socialism that everyone can perform."[1]

With the Hitler salute, the regime intruded into the tiniest elements of everyday life. Postmen used the greeting when they knocked on people's doors to deliver packages or letters. Customers entering department stores were greeted with "Heil Hitler, how may I help you?" Dinner guests brought, as house gifts, glasses etched with the words "Heil Hitler"; children were given three-inch-tall plastic figures with pivoting right arms; and print shops turned out millions of copies of photographer Heinrich Hoffmann's famous portrait of the Führer.

That photograph adorned living-room walls in homes throughout Germany, with rare exceptions, like the apartment belonging to the parents of Johannes Rau, who would later become president of the Federal Republic of Germany. In that home, an equally famous image—the 1933 "Day of Potsdam" photograph of Hitler with German President Paul von Hindenburg—had pride of place. From our perspective, the reason Rau's father preferred this photograph of Hitler with the aristocrat and war hero Hindenburg is particularly interesting. The photograph was chosen, Rau reports, for its implicit criticism of Hitler's lack of humility: for once the Führer could be seen shaking hands with and

Hitler making one last bow before the authority of the old elites at the "Day of Potsdam" in March 1933, which was staged to demonstrate the reconciliation of the revolutionary Nazi movement and Old Prussia.

bowing his head before another human being. Yet we should note that for all his reticence to follow the fashions of the day, an attitude typical of German Christian conservatives, the elder Rau nevertheless obeyed the injunction to put one's political loyalties on display even within the confines of the home.[2]

In no area of their lives were Germans exempted from the duty to perform this "bit of practical National Socialism." Everywhere throughout Germany, small metal signs reminding people to use the Hitler salute were posted in public squares, on telephone poles and street lanterns. The greeting became a component of academic rituals from the university down to kindergarten, a compulsory framework for the pedagogical relationship. Kindergarten and primary school teachers had their

A metal sign from the Third Reich, reading "The True German Greets: Heil Hitler!"

pupils say the new greeting over and over until they got it right. At one kindergarten in southwestern Germany, children were taught to raise their hand to the proper height by hanging their lunch bags across the raised arm of their teacher. Pupils were required to say "Heil Hitler!" at the beginning and end of every school period, and the first thing each new class of first graders encountered when they opened their primers was a lesson on how to greet others, replete with pictures of people lining the streets, their arms raised in the Hitler salute. Such scenes were also popular motifs in art class.

The greeting found its way into fairy tales, too, even classics like *Sleeping Beauty*, scenes from which were often painted on school walls. A 1936 book on pedagogy explains the goals of these reinterpretations: "No fairy tale cries out more for ethnic interpretation than *Sleeping Beauty*. . . . In that story, we reexperience our national impotence and reawakening. Hitler is the hero who has rescued our people from sleep of death into which it had sunk under the evil influence of foreign races. The

A painting from a school art class shows people saluting a Nazi parade.

*A wall painting from a German school shows the prince
greeting Sleeping Beauty with the Hitler salute.*

ethnic [*völkisch*] interpretation should be emphasized in subtle
ways that preserve the fairy-tale character of the portrayal of the
maiden and the prince. Freed from the constraints of realism,
the Führer takes center stage as a savior in the guise of a king's
son, the most noble figure in the imagination of children and
early folklore."[3]

Nazi Germany has been described as a "double state"
(Ernst Fraenkel) in which the regular government administration was often superceded by an ad hoc hierarchy that bypassed
legal decision-making avenues and, invoking the authority of
the Führer himself, ruled by decree. Any number of ordinances
and regulations pertaining to the Hitler salute were issued in
this way during the early years of the regime, some of them

coming directly from upper levels of the administration, others formulated by subordinate administrators. For example, the department of education and cultural affairs of the state of Württemberg appended the following language of its own to a July 24, 1933, ordinance decreed by German Interior Minister Wilhelm Frick: "It is hereby ordered that pupils in all schools rise from their seats and offer a raised-arm greeting at the beginning and end of every school day as well as with every change of instructor between periods. During lessons, pupils are required to greet any adult who enters the classroom in the same fashion. Teachers are required to return the greeting. Individual pupils who encounter fellow pupils inside the school building or on school grounds are also required to use the Hitler greeting."

Even before the national edict of July 13 making the Hitler greeting a general civic duty, local authorities were issuing rules of their own. Isa Vermehren, who grew up in a middle-class household in the northern German city of Lübeck and later moved to Berlin to become a cabaret musician, recalled the episode at her high school that contributed to her decision to leave school. On May 1, 1933, which had just been officially declared German Labor Day, "students at all of Lübeck's schools were required to practice the German greeting in their schoolyards. We had to raise our arms, hands outstretched, to eye level and march in rows of eight. Then we all paraded past the stands at the main athletic field. The teachers had assembled there, and lots of flags were flying. As we passed by the flags, we had to raise our arms again. A girl in front had been told that she wasn't allowed to raise her arm because she wasn't an Aryan. That irritated me so much that I thought, If she isn't allowed, I'm not going to either."[4]

Ingeborg Schäfer, the daughter of a senior SS officer in

Danzig, now the city of Gdańsk in Poland, has her own recollections of the "bit of practical National Socialism" as it was carried out in her family: "When my sister and I went for walks through the city with my father, we always fought over who would get to walk on his left. It was uncomfortable to walk on his right. Our father always held our hands to make sure we didn't run off, and he was constantly having to return salutes from other officers. He kept raising his arm, and whichever of us was on his right, fascinated by the impression of the city, seldom let go of his hand in time. Your arm was always being jerked up with his."[5]

There is no shortage of examples like these, illustrating how readily Germans adopted the Hitler salute. But beyond the anecdotes and the regional and religious differences, the question remains: was "Heil Hitler" really a greeting? Wasn't it something else—a communicative practice that merely took the form of a greeting as a means of disguise, a verbal armband, a membership card? Certainly the Hitler salute looked like a greeting and was influenced by the pragmatics and logic of greetings, but in fact it did something more—and other—than greetings normally do.

THE SPOKEN component of the Hitler greeting is usually translated with the deceptively simple "Hail Hitler." Although that was undoubtedly among the meanings conveyed by the phrase "Heil Hitler," its connotations go much further. Just as the English word "hail" is related to its homonym "hale," in the sense of healthy, the German verb *heilen* primarily means "to heal," while the noun *Heil* means happiness or welfare or, in religious contexts, salvation. The matter is further complicated by the fact that it is semantically unclear whether the word *heil* in

"Heil Hitler" is a noun, adjective, or a verb, and, if it is understood as a verb, whether Hitler is its subject or its object.

The phrase "Heil Hitler"—the linguistic kernel of the Hitler salute—uttered firmly as the right arm is extended stiffly from the body with the palm of the hand open and brought to eye level, contains an elliptically formulated wish for well-being. Blessings and appeals fall well within the connotative range of verbal greetings, and, as we have discussed, the original sense of the German word *grüßen*, to greet, included the notion of an appeal, "to bring [the person greeted] to speech." Nonetheless, the combination of this sense of the word *Heil* with the name Hitler sounds strange and jarring. So let us begin with the word *Heil* alone and then consider the phrase as a whole.

If *Heil* is understood to refer to happiness, health, or welfare, then the person whose name follows that word becomes the object of the greeter's wishes. The greeter seeks to take some of the uncertainty out of the imminent encounter by wishing that his interlocutor emerge from this open-ended process physically and mentally unharmed. The wish remains implicit, as it does in phrases like "Good day," where the greeter is in essence saying "I hope you have a good day." Such formulations signal the greeter's availability, his inclination to cooperate with the person he is greeting, and his desire to get the interpersonal exchange off to the best possible start.

When the greeting *heil* is used in the private sphere, it is always followed by the other person's first name and is used only among friends or people who share a sense of community. *Heil* Gustav or *Heil* Dietrich might sound ominous today, in light of Germany's history, but it would be perfectly consistent with other national customs, for instance, the Swiss use of *salut*, which is derived from the Latin *salve*. Moreover, the word *heil* is in fact still used today as a greeting in a variety of specific situations—for example, among German skiers, hunters, and fishermen. In those usages, it articulates the wish that the party being greeted emerge from a potential dangerous activity safe and sound.

There is no need to trace the development of the *heil* greeting in all its particular historical stages. The point is that it expresses a desire for the continued physical integrity and general well-being of the person being greeted, communicating the wish that he or she remain unscathed. In religious contexts, that meaning is amplified; *heil* signifies the condition of being untouched by worldly harm or the effects of human mortality, and it postulates the existence of a divine authority representing happiness or welfare in their pure form—in a word, salvation. When words like *heil* or "hail" are attached to the name of a ruler or of a country, the religious sense carries over, but in such cases either the person whose name is mentioned has to be physically present or else the phrase in question—for example, *Heil Deutschland* or *Heil dem Vaterland* ("Hail to the fatherland")—is being used as a way for a community to proclaim its own cohesion and integrity. But such formulations aren't greetings in the sense of opening gambits intended to initiate human contact. Rather, they function more like farewells, expressing encouragement in the face of an uncertain situation or even a crisis beyond the encounter.

In Germany, the *heil* greeting was first used in the nineteenth century by members of nationalist and Romantic circles. Imbued with an anthropological pessimism that saw human beings as pitted against one another in eternal competition, they were critical of civilization and highly skeptical of modernity and many of its defining features, including the division of labor, industrialization, and class society. An entry in the *Practical Lexicon of Indo-Germanic Antiquity* [*Reallexikon der indogermanischen Altertumskunde*] from 1917 reads: "With the *heil* greeting, one wishes another person unity and health, a wish that is easy to understand in times of never-ending struggle and injury." To greet someone with *Heil* was a political act, a call for "authenticity" in a world beclouded both by class differences and by attempts to paper them over through political and social emancipation. The greeting was particularly popular among youth organizations like the Scouts and back-to-nature movements, both of which had strong reactionary components in Germany.

WHEN THE *heil* formulation is not used with the first name of the person being addressed, but rather with the last name "Hitler," the communicative space shared by the two participants is expanded to include an absent third entity, in this case one from the secular, political world. That shift alters the very meaning of the greeting. As we have already seen in the example of *Grüß Gott* ("Greet God"), when the initiator of a greeting invokes the authority of a third entity to mediate and protect the encounter, it is as though he were expressing a lack of faith in his own ability to manage the inherent uncertainty of the situation. Yet for a third entity to be credited with the power to overcome human limitations and uncertainty, to build a bridge between people and secure the outcome of their encounter, that entity needs to have, by definition, indisputable moral authority. To invoke God in the greeting *Grüß Gott* is to express absolute trust in His power. But how can this be applied to Hitler?

There are two ways we can interpret the phrase "Heil Hitler." Either the greeter is wishing Hitler health and welfare in the presence of the person he is greeting, or the greeter is calling upon Hitler's authority to wish the *recipient* good health and welfare and to bring Hitler to speech. If we spell out the meaning of the greeting in the first instance, the greeter is saying, in effect, "Our encounter is an occasion to wish Hitler good health, and we think of him when we meet each other." But the problem is that if the greeting is understood this way, it has nothing to do with the situation that required the act of greeting in the first place — except when the participants in the greeting already perceive themselves as part of the community represented by Hitler, in which case the exchange of greetings serves to recall that fact.

In the second interpretation, which conforms to the *Grüß Gott* model, Hitler enters the relationship as the mediating third party. Here if we spell out the meaning of the greeting, it would be something like, "May Hitler offer our encounter his blessing, his protection, and his wish that we both emerge unscathed." In essence, the participants would be saying, "May Hitler keep you well and guarantee your welfare." Of course, no human actor can do this unless he has superhuman powers. As suggested above, the wish for well-being that is inherent in secular forms of the *heil* greeting is comprehensible only if it refers to someone who is physically present. The invocation of Hitler as an absent third party, on the other hand, makes sense only if we assume that his name is seen to be a source of timeless values and an authority not subject to human limitations and the laws of nature. The mortal Hitler is thus sacralized and credited with godlike abilities. The participants in the greeting believe in him as they would in God, and they wish each other well by invoking his name.

The incoherencies in both of these readings are inescapable. To say "Heil Hitler" as though one sincerely meant "It is to you, Hitler, that I am wishing salvation," is absurd, since Hitler — to put it simply — isn't there. But to take the phrase to mean "May Hitler heal you" is equally absurd, for human beings do not have such power. These contradictions often became fodder for wit and humor. One joke that made the rounds in the Third Reich has someone being greeted on the street with "Heil Hitler" and responding "What's he got to do with it?" Another familiar standby was to pretend to understand the word *heil* as the imperative form of the transitive verb "to heal" and answer the greeting with, "Am I a doctor?" or *Heil Du ihn!* ("Heal him yourself!")

Given these incoherencies, it should come as no surprise that, in private encounters, "normal" greetings were often used in tandem with the Hitler salute or would immediately follow it. As a rule, with the exception of official ceremonies, Germans usually shook hands or reverted to other traditional greeting habits once they were finished with saying "Heil Hitler." Jokes about the Nazi salute also allowed Germans to reconnect with "normal" German conventions; the absurd linguistic combinations or substitutions involving either or both elements of the new greeting helped to renormalize the old forms. In Alsace-Lorraine, "Heil Hitler" might thus become *Ein Liter* ("One liter") or *Drei Liter* ("Three liters").[6] "It's lucky that Hitler's last name wasn't 'Kräuter,'" cabaret performer Karl Valentin used to quip. "Otherwise we'd have to go around yelling *Heilkräuter* ['medicinal herbs']."[7]

The semantic content of the greeting becomes comprehensible only if one grants Hitler the power to dissolve accepted principles of communication, and here is where the question of Hitler's charisma becomes key. For it was charisma, which mediates human encounters and bridges the distance between the parties involved, that made it possible to conflate the real and the divine, to replace *Grüß Gott* with "Heil Hitler" as Samuel Beckett noted in Regensburg. Through this linguistic substitution, the secular order was sacralized. Hitler became not only the patron saint of the human encounter but also its medium, and in this way superceded reality itself.

THE PHRASE "Heil Hitler" was only one-half of the Nazi salute, and it bears asking why the Nazis felt it had to be accompanied by a raised arm, instead of, as is the case with *Guten Tag,* by a normal shaking of hands. Why, we might ask, was an accompanying gesture necessary at all?

One possible explanation is that physical gestures in greetings serve to emphasize contact, and in fact in the Hitler greeting the hand and arm movements of the person giving the salute seem to be directed toward the recipient, the rising arm and open palm synchronizing the greeter's body with his words and bridging the physical distance between the actors. Handshakes do this, as do waves of greeting or farewell; they can augment the words and echo and enhance the message. Yet in the Hitler salute the arm is not extended toward the person being

A plastic Hitler figurine with raisable right arm.

greeted but beyond him. It points upward into empty space, designating a fictive realm of possible encounter somewhere above the individual being greeted. Like lines of perspective or the beams of searchlights at Nazi Party rallies that shone into the night sky where they met in an infinitely distant beyond, the arms and hands of those giving each other the Hitler salute forever approached each other but never joined. German hands were open, but they made no actual contact.

We can read the gestural component of the Hitler salute in two different ways. An open hand in a gesture of greeting signals that the greeter is not carrying a weapon; it indicates peacefulness of intention, which, as we have seen, is an important aspect of verbal greetings as well. Also significant is the fact that the right arm was the one to be raised, except in case of physical infirmity. Samuel Beckett wrote ironically of the stir that he had caused at a morning concert of an SS band on November 11, 1936: "I stretched the wrong arm to Horst Wessel & Haydn."[8] The right arm has traditionally been seen, in contrast to the left, as representing authenticity and credibility. Yet the raising of the right arm in the Hitler salute does something quite different as well: it makes it necessary for the greeter to stand back from the other person and thus intensifies the estrangement and sense of uncertanty that is usually overcome or bridged during an act of greeting.

The physical component of the Hitler salute was not confined to the hand and the arm. Tension and rigidity throughout the body, indicative of concentration and solemnity, were important elements as well. In this regard, the Hitler greeting resembles the classic military salute, in which physical posture emphasizes hierarchy. In the military salute, a forced solemnity permeates every aspect of the gesture, and the demand for attention on the part of the person giving the salute is so absolute as to make it impossible for him even to think about any other action, particularly one that might disrupt the clear and orderly line of command. When a soldier salutes, he is demonstrating that he is ready, willing, and able to subordinate himself to the chain of command, and the rigidity of his body de-emphasizes, indeed dismisses, the possibility that he might act independently, even to save his own life. The difference between the individual and his role vanishes—an impression that the soldier's uniform, his headgear in particular—reinforces. All of a soldier's physical motions, including his salute, are subordinated to a single, unambiguous goal and must therefore be all of a piece. (Against this backdrop, one can begin to understand why the German *Wehrmacht* held on to its own traditions and did not adopt the Hitler salute in its internal encounters until 1944. The military leadership realized that the Hitler salute was incompatible with the total commitment required of military forces, a topic to which we will return.)

Transferring a ritual of total engagement and absolute commitment to the civilian context of public greetings, as happened in the case of the Hitler salute, implies the subordination of the civic sphere to the norms of hierarchy, asymmetrical by definition. The salute divided all of German society, including civilians, into two groups—those who gave orders and those who obeyed them—which heightened in civilian encounters the threat inherent in any human interchange. It is particularly notable, in light of the military aspect of the heavily masculine associations carried by the Hitler greeting, that women were expected to assume a martial stance as well, and in fact did so. The ambiguity of the greeting comes through in the following entry from the *Handbook of Germanic Lore* [*Handbuch der deutschen Volkskunde*], published during the Third Reich: "The greeting reflects a nation's ethnicity" author E. Grohne wrote, "and the gesture its racial essence. A people will be in good shape politically and culturally as long as its own particular greetings and gestures triumph over pan-European cosmopolitanism. Our fatherland can look confidently toward the future in this regard; the German greeting is a herald of national revival. It is a peaceful gesture that nonetheless retains the right of self-defense."[9]

To outsiders, the gesture often appeared grotesque. Martha Dodd, the daughter of the American ambassador to Nazi Germany, paints a memorable picture of future Nazi Foreign Minister Joachim von Ribbentrop introducing himself to others at an official reception. In her 1939 bestseller *Through Embassy Eyes*, she writes,

> The first time I met von Ribbentrop was at a luncheon we gave at the Embassy. He was tall and slender, with a vague blond handsomeness. Outstanding among all the guests, Ribbentrop arrived in Nazi uniform. Most Nazis came to diplomatic functions in ordinary suits unless the affair was extremely formal. His manner of shaking hands was an elaborate ceremony in itself. He held out his hand, then retreated and held your hand at arm's length, lowered his arm stiffly by his side, then raised the arm swiftly in a Nazi salute, just barely missing your nose. All the time he was staring at you with such intensity you were wondering what new sort of mesmerism he thought he was effecting. The whole ritual was performed with such self-conscious dignity and in such silence

that hardly a word was whispered while Ribbentrop made his exhibitionistic acquaintance with
the guests present. To me the procedure was so
ridiculous I could scarcely keep a straight face.
However, I wanted to see him perform the last de-
tail of his "act" so I approached him, stepped
back, stood silently watching him, eyes pinned on
a distant object in back to keep from laughing,
and felt that I quite ably sensed the unspoken
stage directions! This business he went through at
every small party—the pompousness, the mad-
dening leisureliness, the affectation, of course
attracted the attention of everyone present—as he
no doubt intended.[10]

Dodd's description, bordering on caricature, points to a
further complication in the Hitler greeting: not only did the verbal wish for the other person's well-being require investing a
secular figure with supernatural power, but the display of military readiness in the physical gesture jarred with accepted customs of greeting in nonmilitary situations.

THE ONLY way to reconcile the contradictions inherent in the
Hitler greeting is to understand it as an oath of allegiance, an interpretation made possible by the various roles played by the
greeting: it reminded Germans of their common purpose, symbolized by the Führer; it involved a mutual pledge of loyalty to
the community associated with him; and it was not exclusively a
military salute but extended to all encounters in civil society.
The Hitler salute was thus anything but a greeting—or if it was
a greeting, it was so only by virtue of the situation in which it

was carried out. "Heil Hitler" was a mutual call to readiness, and if this call had to be made and remade day after day, it was for the simple reason that the struggle was imminent and grave. Oaths are by their nature unconditional; they are made to ward off the possibility that the intensity of the relationship they govern will slacken and fall prey to moral weakness or negligence. Swearing an oath moves the commitment to action into a sacred sphere in which the pledge taker never has to reevaluate his intentions and reconsider his oath, even if there is a change in the original circumstances that justified it.

The objection might be raised that a true oath of allegiance is a one-time affair and by definition cannot be repeated. The very fact that "Heil Hitler" was used both to open and to close public encounters would seem to put the Hitler greeting at odds with the structural significance of a proper pledge. An oath that has to be repeated undermines what it is intended to create: a permanent relationship. It is as if the original oath had never been made or else cannot be counted on. Pursuing this line of thought, we might say that the Hitler salute aspired to timelessness and permanence as a way of preventing its own decay; yet, failing to recognize its own historicity, it was a declaration spoken into a historical vacuum. The Hitler greeting was an oath that betrayed its own promise.

Nonetheless, various aspects of how and by whom the Hitler greeting was to be practiced indicate that it was indeed regarded as an oath of allegiance. A memorandum issued on December 4, 1933, by the governor of the state of Hesse to all offices under his jurisdiction instructed government workers and functionaries on the proper way of saluting: they could choose to say "Heil Hitler" or "Heil" or "nothing at all." The memorandum further instructed—and this is crucial—that "no words other than 'Heil Hitler' are to be used in the German greeting."[11]

This stricture is consistent with the usual practice of oath taking. Moreover, Hitler himself rarely gave the salute in the stiff-armed manner, and instead only raised his right hand, as if to receive and acknowledge a pledge of allegiance that would have been ridiculous for him to swear to his own person. Finally, as of 1937, Jews were forbidden to use the greeting. That prohibition underscored both the social exclusivity and implicit sacredness of the gesture. To protect the messianic spell of the greeting from "foreign" contamination its use had to be restricted to privileged members of the racially defined community.

The oath of allegiance to Hitler was intended to do away with the traditional conventions of greeting. In the act of greeting, individuals stage their "public personas," defining themselves as social entities with recognizable affiliations. In light of class divides and other group allegiances in traditional German society, using the Hitler greeting was tantamount to disassembling one's own distinct identity. Instead of coming closer to one another, the participants in the greeting distanced themselves in the very moment of their encounter. They fell under the spell of a mystical force that they themselves called into being and that brought them together in a devotional space of mutual estrangement, one that, paradoxically, created between them a kind of cohesion in their very isolation from each other.

In this way, the Hitlerian charisma became a meaningful presence in people's everyday lives—the central referent in any social exchange, but one that was approachable only in an idealized sense, never in any concrete way. Like other elements of Nazi propaganda, the Hitler greeting may have been aimed at introducing the idea of the Führer's presence into all aspects of Germans' daily existence. But the fascination Germans felt for their leader was based on the fact that, even in his imagined omnipresence, he remained a mystical, alien figure, a mystery in the religious sense. Performing the Hitler greeting was a way of approaching him in his remoteness and apprehending the unattainable mystery.

Wolfgang Neuber was a high school student in Berlin during the Third Reich. His recollection of political instruction at school illustrates the degree to which Germans were encouraged to see Hitler as a deity. "I myself knew the required answers," Neuber writes, "because an uncle of mine had been asked the same trick questions. . . . 'What comes after the Third Reich?' he had been asked, to which he had responded, 'The Fourth.' The teacher then corrected him, 'Listen carefully. The Third Reich is eternal.' 'Where does the Führer live?' he was also asked. 'In the Reich Chancellery?' 'Wrong.' 'In Berchtesgaden?' 'No, wrong as well. He lives in the hearts of all Germans.' "Because I knew the right answers to questions," Neuber concluded, "I had no problems with political instruction."[12] In a similar vein, young school pupils, when required to take their afternoon naps, were told to close their eyes, lay their heads on their desks, and think of Adolf Hitler. Before, God had stood as the higher authority that gave life its meaning; now Adolf Hitler fulfilled that role.

EVEN THOUGH the Hitler salute retained the pragmatic social functions of a greeting, it was closer in essence to the sympathetic rites that anthropologist Marcel Mauss observed in premodern "segmentary" societies—social systems comprising numerous relatively small autonomous groups that generally regulate their own affairs but that periodically come together to form larger groups and, in some senses, may collectively appear to be a single large community. When frequency of contact is limited and individuals are isolated from one another but also dependent upon one another, encounters happen via a procedure that transforms every incipient relationship into a form of commonality. Only in this way can relationships be established at all.

The Hitler greeting brought together key aspects of the Nazi social order. It militarized people's individual identities while subordinating those identities to an overarching hierarchy. It combined hopes for salvation with the promise of a general, moral renewal. Despite its stylized archaic form, the Hitler salute—viewed in the context of the history of greetings—represented the radical modernity of the Nazi order. It was to face-to-face encounters what party rallies were for the masses, providing Germans with the illusion of a magical high power. Introducing an extraordinary element into ordinary, everyday existence, it imbued all human encounters with an air of uncertainty, undermining people's confidence in the reality of their interactions with one another. But this is precisely what made it possible for the belief in the Führer's messianic power and a sense of duty to him to be transferred from one person to another in the greeting exchange. Embedded within the everyday performance of routine practices, like a kind of verbal and gestural identity card, the greeting defined and determined Germans' perception of reality so forcefully that expressing doubt on that score came to be seen as a far-fetched proposition, somehow beyond the pale. In this way, the greeting worked automatically to suppress ethical qualms and foster indifference toward the moral implications of the practice itself.

CHAPTER FIVE

The Rise of the Sphere of Mistrust

DIARIES, JOURNALS, AND OTHER AUTOBIOGRAPHICAL writings from the National Socialist period suggest that the Germans' embrace of the Hitler greeting reflected their acceptance of the Nazi system, and that this acceptance in turn resulted from the wish to overcome the crisis in national self-confidence that occurred in the wake of Germany's defeat in World War I and the punitive terms of the Treaty of Versailles. Without a doubt, the general expectation that the charismatic Führer would reverse Germany's national humiliation helped convince Germans of every milieu to sweep aside traditional social rules, including those governing greeting customs. Still, acceptance of the new greeting was neither immediate nor universal, and even outward acceptance of the duty did not imply uncomplicated internal assent.

Let us take a look for a moment at the context in which the greeting arose and the milieu for which it served as a sign of loyalty—the community, or rather, the gang, that grouped itself around Adolf Hitler. Nazism in its early days was a weakly organized movement, a motley assemblage of interests combining *völkisch*, nationalist, and socialist elements held together primarily by marches and other uniformed displays on the streets. The Hitler greeting functioned both as an expression of commitment within the party and as a demonstrative statement to the outside world. It served the further function of asserting the legitimacy of Hitler's leadership against the claims of his early competitors. Hitler's leadership, based as it was on something as intangible and subjective as charisma, was permanently at risk: its validity had to be reaffirmed at every opportunity so that his successes would be perceived as proof of his objective talents. It could not stand up to rational examination or questioning and maintained itself through blind obedience. Yet in spite of this demand for unquestioning obedience, or perhaps because of it, the drive to gain acceptance for the "Heil Hitler" greeting did not go unchallenged, even within the movement.

Early objections focused on its resemblance to its immediate historical predecessor, the *saluto romano* that Benito Mussolini had introduced in Fascist Italy—although the main influence on the young Hitler was not *Il Duce* but Georg von Schönerer, the leader of the anti-Semitic Pan-German (*Alldeutsche*) Party in turn-of-the-century Austria.[1] The raised arm of the *saluto romano* was an explicitly antibourgeois gesture, intended to underscore Mussolini's claim to leadership by connecting it with the Roman Empire.[2]

The legitimacy of the Nazi salute—the "Fascist salute" as some of its detractors within the party called it—was challenged again and again on the grounds that it was not Germanic, and in response efforts were made to establish its pedigree, to invent for it a tradition after the fact. Hitler's deputy

Rudolf Hess argued, falsely, that the Hitler greeting had been a Nazi custom since the earliest days of the movement. In an article titled "The 'Fascist' Greeting," published in the monthly supplement to the *Völkischer Beobachter* in June 1928, Hess opined:

> The NSDAP's introduction of the raised-arm greeting approximately two years ago still gets some people's blood boiling. Its opponents suspect . . . the greeting of being un-Germanic. They accuse it of merely aping the Fascists and snipe that it would have been better to hold to the military custom of raising one's hand to one's cap and other such nonsense. Let us take a closer look at the greeting and the objections to it. Raising the arm is the most natural way to greet. For example, when children and adults greet people speeding past them in their cars, their reflexive response is precisely the gesture just described. . . . As early as 1921, long before we had heard anything about the Fascists and their greeting, our leaders were saluted by the ranks with a raising of the right arm, as a part of the natural reflex mentioned above. And even if the decree concerning greetings from two years ago [Hess's own order that all party members use it] is seen as an adaptation of the Fascist gesture, is that really so terrible? Bolshevism has spread its symbols across the globe. The symbols and secret signs of Freemasonry are used throughout the world and by members of all races. Now the various warriors

of nationalism, organized along the lines of their
respective nations, display those elements they
have in common, as well as their alliance in the
struggle against mutual international enemies,
through a common greeting practice.

Two elements of Hess's argument stand out: one is the desire
to distance the Hitler greeting from the raised fist of the Socialist
International—a gesture derided as a sign of choleric impa-
tience; the other is the subordination of national particularisms
to the more important goal of fighting a common enemy.

German skepticism about the *saluto romano* had its coun-
terpart in claims by the Italian Fascists, who believed themselves to be the only legitimate inheritors of the tradition of

*"The German greeting"
versus the* saluto
romano—*Hitler meets
Mussolini.*

Imperial Rome. As for the *saluto romano* itself, although it, like the Hitler salute, was used in everyday greetings, the physical gesture was not accompanied by any standard utterance. It was, however, enhanced with an additional physical component in February 1938, when Mussolini made the Fascist goosestep, or *passo romano*, mandatory for all military parades. Justifying the edict, Mussolini wrote, "We want to introduce military discipline because we are convinced that without it Italy will never become the Mediterranean and global nation of which we dream. Those who accuse us of marching like the Germans should note that it's not we who are copying from them. On the contrary, it's the Germans who have copied and keep copying the Romans. We're the ones returning to our origins, to our original Roman, Latin, and Mediterranean style."[3] The particular features of the Italian greeting were that it was class oriented, calling to mind Mussolini's socialist origins, and remained verbally neutral, whereas the German version was *völkisch* and comprised gesture and words in tight connection.

Academic attempts to legitimize the Hitler salute began as early as 1933, with the first laws mandating its use throughout public life. Ethnologists and ethnographers struggled to work out what was "authentically Germanic" about it. Their efforts sometimes inspired satirical verse, like this bit of student doggerel:

> *The old Germanic tribesmen on both banks of the*
> *   Rhine*
> *Lay spread out bearskins, drinking their wine,*
> *When, with German greeting, a Roman entered*
> *   their midst*
> *"Heil Hitler, you Germans, 'tis I—Tacitus."*

The greeting faced other challenges as well. Acceptance of the Hitler salute in Germany's Protestant north was widespread and strong—"Children, big and small, no longer say 'Good morning, Mother' or 'Good night, Father' but rather only 'Heil Hitler,'" noted one Hamburg society matron in her diary—but in the historically Catholic south the greeting received a more mixed reception.[4] The apparent regional divide was ironic, given the fact that the Nazi movement had originated in the south, in Munich, but it was not inexplicable. The sheer number of sites in Munich commemorating the rise of the party meant that nowhere else were Germans so often required to give the Hitler salute. But this in turn meant more occasions for people there to *avoid* the obligation, and that they did, so much so that some critics nicknamed Munich the "capital of the *Grüß Gott* movement." Even today, the city's *Viscardigasse* is known to locals as "Shirkers' Alley" since people who wanted to bypass the *Feldherrnhalle*, the site of Hitler's attempted Beer Hall Putsch of 1923, used to take that narrow street to avoid having to salute this Nazi holy site.

To judge from secret-police reports, Germans had grown lax about performing the greeting quite early on, but displaying a casual attitude toward it remained a risky proposition, as enforcement of the proper greeting could be violent. Berlin resident Ingeborg Schneider Lütschow recalled, "It must have been around '34 or '35, and my father went out to get something in the Charlottenburg district. . . . As he was waiting on the sidewalk with a group of others to cross the street, a troop of Hitler Youths marched up. It was a group of fifteen- to seventeen-year-old boys led by a standard bearer. The next thing my father knew he was feeling the sting of a seventeen-year-old hand on his cheek. One of the Hitler Youths had slapped him, and all the other men and women around him, too, because, as the young Nazi said, 'the pigs' hadn't promptly saluted the flag."[5]

Sometimes the reactions were not merely violent but plainly bizarre, as we can see in a July 23, 1934, memo sent to local police stations by the Ministerial Division 1A of the Hessian State Government: "There have been reports of traveling vaudeville performers training their monkeys to give the German greeting on command at the end of performances. Displays of this sort make a mockery of the German greeting and are liable to provoke public disorder. We therefore order you to keep an eye on all vaudeville shows in your municipality and, in case of violations, to see to it that said animals are destroyed." There is no way of knowing whether the trained monkeys were

Making "a mockery of the German greeting," vaudeville performer Traubert Petter (left) and his chimpanzee Moritz.

intended as a parody of the state's "training" of its citizenry or as an expression of their owners' support for the regime. In any case, once the act of greeting had become a political sacrament, a sacred oath of allegiance to Hitler, the animals were obviously guilty of profanation, and only through their sacrifice could the sin be expiated.[6]

NOT SURPRISINGLY, outright resistance met with the strongest reactions. The "Law to Prevent Insidious Attacks on the State and the Party, and to Protect Party Uniforms," issued on December 20, 1934, and the special courts that were set up at the same time to prosecute violators, laid down the institutional legal foundations for enforcing the greeting. But in fact the Reich had been persecuting individuals who refused to perform the Hitler salute since 1933. One of the most prominent victims was the Protestant clergyman Paul Schneider, the "Iron-Willed Preacher of Buchenwald," who was imprisoned for refusing to use the greeting in confirmation instruction, for displaying material critical of the regime's race policies on the bulletin board outside his church, and for preaching sermons that encouraged Germans to resist Hitler. He died in 1939, having been beaten, tortured, and finally poisoned after refusing earlier that year to salute the swastika flag on Hitler's birthday.[7]

Not all who opposed the greeting did so directly; many took a more cautious approach and tried to navigate their way through or around it, with varying results. Viktor Klemperer's diaries record a conversation with Martin Bollert in 1937, after the latter had resigned from his post as director of the Saxon State Library in Dresden. Bollert complained about the difficulty of having to conform to Nazi regulations while trying to stay true to one's moral principles. "You won't believe how few [true] National

Socialists there are. So many people come to see me. First with their arm stretched out, Hitler salute. Then they feel their way into the conversation. Then, when they've become certain, the mask falls. I, too, have to raise my arm. I say 'Heil'—but I cannot utter 'Heil Hitler.' I was just in southern Germany. There you only seldom hear 'Heil Hitler.' Mostly it's *'Grüß Gott.'*"[8]

Carlo Schmid, who would later become a Social-Democratic member of parliament in the Federal Republic, was blocked from promotion in his job at the University of Tübingen in 1933, after he was repeatedly observed responding to the Hitler greeting by tipping his hat. Werner Finck, a Berlin cabaret performer, was banned from the stage after starting off a show with the words "Heil . . . um, how does the rest of it go?" Johannes Rau tells of a pastor from Wuppertal, Karl Immer, who habitually responded to

Richard Strauss, 1943, at the celebration ceremony in the Vienna Rathaus of "five years of Hitler in Austria."

the Hitler greeting by solemnly giving his own last name. It was an ambivalent act, which could be seen as affirming the greeting, since *immer* means "always," but also allowed the pastor to remain true to the old bourgeois custom of answering a greeting by saying one's surname.

At schools, colleges, and universities, which made the greeting mandatory early on, students gauged their teachers' loyalty toward the regime from the way they saluted. Author Erhard Eppler recalled, for instance, a teacher of his, Herr Storz: "We knew where all our teachers stood toward the party," Eppler wrote, "and we didn't have to check whether they were wearing an insignia. We got a clearer indication from the way in which they performed the mandatory Hitler greeting. Storz would sometimes make an arm motion that, in a generous interpretation, could just barely pass for a salute; but then after a moment's silence, he would always say 'Good morning.'"[9] Herman Schwerbrock of the Laurentius-Gymnasium in Warendorf made a list of the various physical and verbal contortions that teachers performed so as to finesse the obligation. Some would lower their eyes shamefully to the floor as they extended their arm, or would hold a piece of chalk in their hand as they raised it and then immediately begin writing on the blackboard. Others appeared in class with heavy piles of books under their arms so as to make saluting impossible.

Even for those who resisted the greeting indirectly or accommodated themselves to it halfheartedly, there was a price to pay in terms of self-respect. Moreover, compromises of the sort just described, which pitted an institutional demand for conformity against the individual's commitment to his moral principles, transformed the sphere of public communications and profoundly affected the social climate. Viktor Klemperer,

Pictures of Germans saluting Hitler from first-grade penmanship exercise books.

in a diary entry from June 13, 1934, writes of "fearful silence, mutual mistrust, and burdensome constraint."[10] Author Thomas Wolfe, who attended the 1936 Olympic Games as an enthusiastic fan, wrote in his novel *You Can't Go Home Again*:

Else turned and surveyed Heilig coldly and sternly. Heilig answered her look with a stare that was equally unrelenting and hostile. There was a formidable quality in the mutual suspicion they displayed as their eyes met. George had observed the same phenomenon many times before in the encounters of Germans who were either total strangers or who did not know each other well. At once their defenses would be up, as if each distrusted the other on sight and demanded full credentials and assurances before relenting into any betrayal of friendliness and confidence. George was used to this sort of thing by now. It was what was to be expected. Just the same, it never failed to be alarming to him when it happened. He could not accustom himself to it and accept it as an inevitable part of life, as so many of these Germans seemed to have done, because he had never seen anything like it at home, or anywhere else in the world before."[11]

Sociologist René König described the generally oppressive atmosphere in a letter to the philosopher Karl Löwith of June 1937:

The gloom, the lethargy, the resignation . . . all of it has become so common that people believe they are suffocating. Flaccidity has become a general character trait as people suffer under the constant need to find compromises. Compromises are sought even when they're not necessary. The result is a state of lazy hypocrisy such as affects even the best of people if they lack the courage to isolate themselves. You can't even morally condemn this state of mind as hypocritical because to be truly hypocritical, you have to do something in a positive sense, and that's seldom the case. What we have is a general state of people letting themselves go, a moral transgression that consists of failing to do the right thing."[12]

HUMAN ENCOUNTERS begin in uncertainty, and it is the function of the greeting exchange to address that uncertainty by bridging the distance between two individuals, by providing them access to each other. But when the greeting is externally imposed and mechanically performed, when it hides rather than reveals, uncertainty in the face of the unknown gives way to mistrust in the face of the unknowable. As Wolfe and König suggest, the mistrust engendered by the Hitler greeting gave it a pernicious power. It restricted people's options in presenting themselves to others, which in turn restricted the options of others in adapting to them or to the encounter. The German greeting, invoking Hitler as a transcendent protective presence, was a defensive gesture that created distance even as it putatively spanned the divide. In this way, it helped pave the way for the individual's self-negation in the ostensible moment of his self-assertion.

Mistrust combined with a readiness to denounce others formed a sinister hybrid that grew in the rotting soil of a languishing social sensibility. The very idea of social reciprocity, based as it is on mutual acceptance, became warped, for the simple reason that no one knew anymore whom he was dealing with. People limited their social contacts and retreated into trusted, reliable circles of family and friends. Under these circumstances, a culture of universal suspicion flourished, as is reflected in a rash of Nazi laws, including the "Reich President's Decree on Defense Against Insidious Attacks upon the Government of National Uprising" (March 21, 1933), the "Law to Prevent Insidious Attacks on the State and the Party, and to Protect Party Uniforms" (December 20, 1934), and the "Decree Concerning Special Criminal Law in War and Special Assignments" (August 17, 1938).

In *Tadellöser und Wolff,* an autobiographical novel set in the northern German city of Rostock, author Walter Kempowski recounts a scene in which his mother tried to convince the gestapo of the innocence of her Danish son-in-law, who, having been seen dressed in black on the day German troops invaded Denmark, had come under suspicion. Kempowski depicts his mother as saying: " 'The Danes loved their king and everything connected with him. Passionately. Just as we love our Führer or, earlier, you in your youth loved the Kaiser.' . . . The gestapo man then got up and went to the window. 'Frau Kempowski,' he said, 'you have no idea how many bad people there are. Germany is crawling with spies.' "[13]

At the start of World War II in September 1939, Nazi authorities posted small signs in train carriages and public squares reading "Watch what you say! The Enemy is listening!" The self-censorship that resulted merely from knowing that one could attract suspicion was enough to change the climate of communication.

Ultimately, what made it possible for Germans to accept the Hitler greeting was neglect, an attitude in turn made possible by a perception of society that so attenuated people's expectations of social exchange they became indifferent to the presence of others. Human encounters no longer held out the prospect of individuals coming together in common, practical action. The greeting became a distancing ritual initiating a relationship of mistrust and disregard. In many cases, discrimination began the first time someone crossed the street on seeing a Jewish neighbor coming their way. Such acts of avoidance reflected a loss of trust in social situations, in the possibility of self-expression, and in one's perception of others. The breakdown in social values, which found its perfect expression in the crass ritual of the Hitler greeting, systematically preceded the practice of ideological exclusion.

Germany's path to the extermination camps, as we know, required the normative construction of the Other, the naturalization of that construction, and the social expulsion of those who were so categorized. But it also required transformation of an entire society into a sphere of mistrust, which in this case came about through the deactivation of two operations fundamental to the formation of social relations—anticipating the future and reflecting on the past—such that they could no longer function as a means of overcoming uncertainty. Anticipating the future as a space of potential action is possible only when we can look back and reflect on the past as a space in which we and others have already acted; an awareness of and trust in the present requires both.

Conversely, when mistrust sets the tone in the social sphere, rules of civility no longer make sense, and people become increasingly willing to accept radical breaks with ethical norms, indeed outright barbarity. Germans' mistrust toward others with whom they came into direct contact and their fragile faith in a sacral presence—their imagined and unattainable

relationship with a charismatic leader—were mutually rein-
forcing. Other human beings were simultaneously present and
absent. One encountered them while remaining completely
distant, and, because the leader's charisma required that he remain forever out of reach, people set their sights elsewhere still,
on an unworldly, transcendent closeness that superceded the
presence and dignity of the people they actually encountered.
In the sacralized social order of the Nazi regime, people came
to define themselves in a radically altered way. They became
tools, vessels for the will of the leader, their god.

CHAPTER SIX

Devaluing the Present

How did Germans come to accept the National Socialist regime? Historical approaches to this question generally focus on external conditions, the economic situation in which the Germans found themselves, as well as what Max Weber called their "inner destiny." Their nation's defeat in World War I had humiliated them, the ensuing economic crisis damaged them financially, and they had lost confidence in the Weimar Republic and its procedural democracy. People from all classes felt an enormous sense of betrayal and began to long for a savior who would ease their burdens.

Although none of these motivations can be discounted, they don't help explain how social rules as basic as those governing the greeting could have dissolved to such an extent, and so early in the game, even before ministerial decrees made the use of the Hitler greeting mandatory. Nor do they help answer questions raised by the fact that the "Heil Hitler" ritual was in essence an oath of loyalty to a charismatic leader: How did

Germans come to place their trust in a single public figure? Was it even to Hitler himself, the concrete individual, that this trust was directed? What can account for a disconnection of private morality and the public sphere so radical that people came to mistrust nearly all of the values that had previously guided their lives and either isolated themselves from the moral contradictions around them or drowned out the voice of their own conscience in ceaselessly repeated demonstrations of loyalty?

In the case of Hitler and, more specifically, through the incessant invocation of his authority in the act of greeting, Germans so internalized the promise of salvation—of heaven on earth—that they came to feel that loyalty (*Gefolgschaft*) was their duty, apart from any threat of external sanctions. Allegiance now meant participation in what had become a sacralized reality, and moral scrutiny of one's own actions became superfluous.

As for charisma, which displayed its power in the Hitler salute, it should not be mistaken for popularity in the usual sense, or even the contagious appeal of the pop idol. Charisma is rather, as Max Weber understood, a "revolutionary force" that unleashes "a change of direction in people's beliefs and actions as part of a complete reorientation of attitudes toward every individual form of life and indeed the world itself."[1] This reorientation can redefine even those relationships which, by virtue of following their own inner logic, had once been thought inviolable. The Hitler salute—which, as both oath and greeting, combined the solemn with the ordinary, the sacred with the everyday, in a way that went unnoticed—is a prime example of the reorientation that Weber describes. The internalized sense of community, reconceived as a sacred entity, was expected to replace existing social differentiations.

We must therefore turn our attention to various German institutions and the communities they formed. We need to consider their internal ritual structure and the particular ways in which they constituted themselves as collectivities. Accepting or rejecting the Hitler greeting was not purely a matter of personal inclination or character but rather was conditioned by the institutions within which Germans lived and which they were willing to abandon in order to follow the new order. What concerns us is not so much the structure of the many associations, political parties, and clubs per se — the so-called intermediary groups into which the population distributed itself according to professional, social, and class interests — but rather how those groups understood themselves culturally and, in particular, how they perceived their internal social interactions. With Hitler's seizure of power, all institutions found themselves under pressure; the charismatic avant-garde, flush with its recent political successes, posed an imminent threat to their very existence. Under pain of heavy sanctions, their members had to swear allegiance to the Führer and, along with everyone else, accept him as the new point of reference. They were challenged at the core of their moral sensibilities.[2]

The Hitler greeting functioned in this context as a way of extending the authority of the Nazi order from a particular community of believers to a host of other institutional spheres. It was like the opening gambit in a game of chess, which allows the two sides to begin testing each other. As an expression of a sacralized community, the Hitler greeting challenged those areas of German society that had their own established traditions governing human interaction. But the game was fixed. The sacralization of secular society in its entirety necessarily limited people's possibilities for acting on their own internal, traditional ideas.

The more the Führer principle took hold as the major determinant of personal relations, social interactions, and national solidarity, the more Germany's established institutions lost their ability to maintain their internal autonomy and uphold their own rules. Institutional cultures disintegrated, along with their specific communicative norms, and people succumbed to the temptation to withdraw from the communities that had formed around these institutions. Germans may have justified this retreat into indifference as an act of self-preservation, but in the end it had the opposite effect and permanently crippled their ability to act in the public sphere. Ethical considerations grew more and more limited in their purview, and the connection between private and public virtues was severed. As the secular world was made sacral, the tension between the present and the future — that is, between action and consequence — lost its moral relevance.

The institutions with the most to tell us about the process by which Germans accepted the Hitler greeting are precisely those that, owing to their specific forms of communication and particular traditions of autonomy, should have been the ones most likely to resist it: the church, the military, and the family. The church is of interest for two reasons — the doctrine of the equality of all people in the eyes of God, so central in Christian thought, and the distinction made in Christian liturgy and ritual between the law of the state and the will of God. The military is significant because of the pragmatic nature of its institutional mission toward which all of its own internal rituals, hierarchies, and rules of interpersonal contact were geared. The family is important, not only for its role in centralizing, articulating, and transmitting criteria of moral acceptability — a role it shares with educational institutions in the formal sense — but also for the particular way the question of Nazi allegiance played itself out there. The pedagogical authority of schools derived from compulsory education laws—in other words, was consonant with the interests of the state—whereas the family represented a separate sphere which, because of its paternalistic structure, found itself in competition with the Führer principle and its sacralized demands upon individual obedience.

THE HITLER greeting and the values it conveyed posed a particular threat to religious communities, given their organization as so-called total institutions. Total institutions, structures that claim the right to complete control over the actions of their adherents, expect absolute acceptance of their social norms and reject competing moral goals as incompatible with their values—in the case of religious institutions, the values of a community dedicated to the spiritual salvation of the world. The Jehovah's Witnesses, for example, who endeavor to lead morally exemplary lives in anticipation of that end, considered the phrase "Heil Hitler" blasphemous and were ruthlessly persecuted. Similar, if less drastic, conflicts arose between Nazism and the moral values of Germany's mainline faiths—Protestantism and Catholicism. The conflicting claims of secular political systems and the religious order inevitably create tension between worldly and church allegiances. The rise of Hitler's charismatic leadership, with its promise of salvation here on earth, challenged the churches to assert their own domain of institutionally protected values.[3]

The Protestant Lutheran church and Germany's Catholic church adapted—and compromised—in ways that reflected their different statuses as national church and minority religion, respectively. Each faith, it bears remembering, also produced its own heroes who resisted the general selling-out of the church's authority. The bishop of Münster, Count Clemens August von Galen, was one of the most vocal Catholic figures of resistance, speaking out against Nazi euthanasia policies and the party's hostility toward the church. The leading figures on the Protestant side were the pastors Karl Barth and Dietrich Bonhoeffer. Barth's refusal to declare allegiance to Hitler in 1935 and to begin his lectures in theology with the Hitler greeting led to his dismissal from his post as professor of theology at the University of Bonn and his subsequent return to his native Switzerland. (His departure was a heavy blow for Germany's Protestant community, which was already in crisis, torn apart by the issue of political conformism.) Bonhoeffer, who remained in Germany, founded the alternative Confessing Church, an illegal organization that tirelessly criticized Nazi anti-Semitism and helped Jews escape Germany. He was executed by the Nazis in 1945, a few weeks before the end of World War II.

In a letter to his friend Emil Brunner, Barth sarcastically quoted the expert theological opinion commissioned by the state prosecutor's office as part of its effort to strip him of his professorship, which in Germany was a civil service position. "What the Cologne prosecutor's office accused me of," wrote Barth, "will interest you as a matter of recent religious history. 'Whether the loyalty and obedience demanded of civil servants is in harmony with God's commandments . . . this is not a matter to be decided by individual civil servants, but rather by the Führer himself, whom God elevated to that position and in whom we must blindly trust. We must believe that because of his special relationship to God the Führer would never demand of his subjects anything that God has forbidden. The sense behind the oath of loyalty to the Führer's person is that the civil servant shall have limitless and uncompromising faith in the Führer and entrust him solely with the decision as to whether there are any discrepancies between his orders and commands and God's will.' "[4]

Catholics, as members of a religious minority, had always tended to form a subculture and were immune at first to the allures of National Socialism. This initial resistance eroded as more and more Catholics embraced the Nazi idea of popular community (*Volksgemeinschaft*), which they saw as a chance to end centuries of anti-Catholic discrimination by the Protestant majority. Hitler's government concluded a concordat with the Vatican on July 20, 1933, which nominally guaranteed the autonomy of the Catholic church in Germany, and despite periodic government harassment, German Catholics increasingly came to believe in the Führer's promise of neutral policies that would end the traditional inequality between the Protestant and Catholic communities.

German Protestantism, by contrast, was highly factionalized, the divisions tending to fall along regional lines. As we saw in the preceding chapter in the case of Pastor Paul Schneider, Protestant churches for the most part incorporated the Hitler greeting into religious instruction and refrained from taking a public stand against the regime. In 1933, the Protestant church in the eastern region of Thuringia had its clergymen read the following declaration, signed by the regional bishop, from their pulpits: "Out of a world mired in lies and deception, a people must arise to take up the standard of Christ and carry forth His message—faith in God and in His shining empire. As we swear loyalty to Germany's God-given leader, our belief in the vanquishing power of the savior of all mankind arises in triumph."

Abbot Alban Schachleiter performs a compromise salute, halfway between a blessing and a Hitler greeting.

To understand how Germany's Protestant and Catholic churches adapted to the Nazi regime, we need to bracket their differences and the isolated acts of resistance by a few heroic individuals and set out in broad terms the common basic orientation of these two main branches of German Christianity. For bound up with their immediate institutional religious function of providing spiritual direction and purpose were conceptions of reality whose particular ways of apprehending temporality are important for our analysis. At issue is something as basic and essential as people's understanding of the purpose of human existence on earth. What Protestantism and Catholicism share, with their distinction between the imperfection of this world and future redemption, is a conception of the present as a time of testing, a period of trial.

And so, let us return to the greeting. As we have said, when someone greets another person, he sets out a relationship to him, declares himself present spatially and temporally, opens himself to the other person, and recalls the state of mutual dependence that is the context for all human exchange. But the Hitler greeting did not do any of these things. How, then, did its distortion of these essential greeting functions square with Christian perceptions of the present? We are not concerned with the historical, philosophical, or theological roots of these perceptions but rather their implications.[5] What does it mean to say that Christianity apprehends the present as a time of testing, and what becomes of the moral status of the experience of the moment from this perspective? In a trivial sense, of course, one's existence on earth is always a test, and the present its temporal dimension, but what is particular about the Christian perspective is the nature of the stakes involved—nothing less than salvation or damnation, and for all eternity. If the test is understood in this way, then the present, rather than merely being experienced as potentiality, constitutes a threat—for the simple reason that tests can be failed.

Protestantism and Catholicism deal with the threat in two different ways, by ascribing different meanings to the present, both of which serve to erase it. Protestantism shifts ultimate judgments of the moral quality of individual actions out of the present and into the future. Good deeds done in the here and now neither bring about nor even indicate future salvation, which depends on a grace that God bestows and that no human being can know or alter. The moral significance of the present must await the Day of Judgment, and it is only then that the moral worth of an individual's actions is revealed to him; the present thus becomes irrelevant, even completely meaningless. Actions seem to take place without the individual's agency, and the application of normal ethical criteria to human behavior is postponed. The result can be a kind of moral blindness.

In Catholicism, on the other hand, it is not the future that eclipses the present but rather the past, for it is only in reference to what has come before that human action acquires its moral significance. For the Catholic church, moral standards were set by God, announced by Christ, and entrusted to the church and its hierarchy to pass on to future generations. Individuals can confront the present and its moral demands unreflectively. They are relieved of autonomous responsibility for shaping their own actions, knowing that their salvation is assured so long as they faithfully abide by received precepts and inherited customs, as presented to them by their spiritual directors.

Both Protestantism, in deferring final moral reckoning to the future, and Catholicism, by anchoring moral meaning so confidently to the past, fed a tendency to avoid the ethical burdens of the present. They shifted the question of what it means to act morally forward and backward respectively, privileging attitudes toward the present that were distant, vacuous, and arrogantly disengaged. It is precisely these sorts of conceptions of time that gave plausibility to the notion of Hitler's quasi-divine providence that underlay the Nazi greeting. Providence is nothing more than temporality without participation; what happens in the world can be attributed to a social cause that obviates the need for individual personal initiative and occludes any accompanying moral reflections.

Although pastors and priests never went so far as to give the Hitler greeting from the pulpit or incorporate it into liturgical practice, Germany's two largest religious communities provided little effective resistance to the Nazi reshaping of social mores. Barth perhaps put it best, when he wrote, sarcastically, from Swiss exile, "In the area of bringing [Germans] into line [with Nazism], there have been the greatest and most majestic miracles. I would hardly be surprised if one day our canaries or turtles lifted their feet to give the Hitler salute and raised their voices to say the accompanying 'Heil.'"

THE MILITARY was another institutional realm with its own clearly defined domain. It had its own hierarchy, command structure, and rules of conduct, all of which were directed toward its specific purposes. Although German generals supported the policies of the regime, the party's demands for their absolute loyalty came into conflict with their duty as soldiers. On one side were the paramilitary SA and the SS, which were party institutions with their own political ambitions, each seeking dominance and autonomy. On the other side was the *Wehrmacht*, with its institutionalized, political duty to be ever ready for military interventions. Use of the Hitler salute became one of the central issues defining relations between the state, or party, and the military under the Reich. The military leadership managed for a long time to retain its own traditional customs and independent internal chain of command and refused to adopt the Hitler salute. But when Hitler assumed the presidency, in addition to the German chancellorship, after Hindenburg's death in 1934, the military swore an oath of loyalty to the Führer, and it was agreed that members of the military and representatives of state authority would recognize each other's protocols for saluting. An edict from the Reich Defense Ministry of September 19, 1933, spelled out the terms of the compromise:

There will be no change in previous forms of military greeting for soldiers on duty, regardless of whether they are in uniform or in athletic clothing and independent of whether they are wearing headgear. The German greeting is used by soldiers and uniformed civil servants in the following situations, a) while singing the national anthem and the *Horst Wessel Lied*; and b) in nonmilitary encounters both within and outside of the *Wehrmacht*. In written communication with government offices and individuals there are no objections to replacing longer formulations with the increasingly common "Heil Hitler!"[6]

The institutional autonomy of the military, which would hold on to its own salute until 1944, quickly evaporated with this decision, as modification of the military oath of loyalty demonstrates.

Until 1933, members of the military swore their oath of allegiance in the following words: "I swear by God this sacred vow that I will faithfully and truly serve my people and my country at all times, and that I will be prepared as a brave and obedient soldier to be ever willing to risk my life to uphold this vow." In 1934, the wording was changed to: "I swear by God this sacred vow that I will offer my unqualified obedience to the leader of the German Empire and the German people, Adolf Hitler, the commander-in-chief of the military, and that I will be prepared as a brave soldier to be ever willing to risk my life to uphold this vow."

And so the personal bond to the Führer was forged. The new oath, whose consequences few envisioned at the time, and the circumstances in which it came about shed light on the moral conflict faced by members of the German resistance in 1944. After the failed attempt to assassinate Hitler on July 20, 1944, which was led by *Wehrmacht* officers, the commanders of the three main branches of the German military—desperate to prove their loyalty—asked the Führer to personally approve their decision to introduce the Hitler greeting within the *Wehrmacht* itself. The change was officially instituted on July 24, 1944, completing the destruction of the military's auton-omy that had commenced a decade earlier with the new loyalty oath. The story of the military's piecemeal capitulation belies arguments made after the war that Germany's armed forces maintained significant distance from the ambitions of the po-litical decision makers in Berlin.

FINALLY WE turn our attention to the family—the sphere to which people retreat from the trials of public and professional life to pursue their private interests. The family is particularly significant as a social institution because the relationship be-tween parents and children is crucial for the development of a specific moral perspective; the family is where most people first acquire the ethical criteria necessary for judgment in the public sphere as well. Sebastian Haffner, one of Germany's most per-ceptive chroniclers of the Third Reich, saw the private, familial sphere as key to understanding Germans' sudden and seem-ingly inexplicable acceptance of the Nazi regime. Behind that acceptance, Haffner wrote in his autobiography, there were

> some very peculiar, very revealing mental processes
> and experiences. You cannot come to grips with
> them if you do not track them down to the place

where they happen: the private lives, emotions, and thoughts of individual Germans. They happen there all the more since, having cleared the sphere of politics of all opposition, the conquering, ravenous state has moved into formerly private spaces in order to clear these, too, of any resistance or recalcitrance and to subjugate the individual. There, in private, the fight is taking place in Germany. You will search for it in vain in the political landscape, even with the most powerful telescope. Today the political struggle is expressed by the choice of what a person eats and drinks, whom he loves, what he does in his spare time, whose company he seeks, whether he smiles or frowns, what he reads, what pictures he hangs on his walls. It is here that the battles of the next world war are being decided in advance.[7]

Essential to understanding the tendency of Germans to withdraw into moral self-isolation during the Third Reich is their conception of the family as a locus of cooperation, allegiance, and mutual support. When Germany entered the modern era, family relations were characterized by a sense of great loyalty. For Germans, the family was the keystone that allowed the individual to integrate himself into the edifice of society; a German's self-respect was intimately connected with—and limited to—his unquestioned feelings of belonging to the family unit, an almost physical sense of transgenerational continuity. It is out of this self-contained world that moral criteria for judging professional, political, and public life emerged: whatever happened outside the four walls of the family home was seen by comparison as less dignified, potentially corrupt, and, in any case, an unlikely arena for the exercise of personal responsibility and competence.

The desire of the younger generation to break from tradition and lead more autonomous lives has always been countered and even suppressed by familial and social pressures to conform. The reason is not any particular hostility to modernity and change, but rather the belief that love, marriage, and family are far and away the best, if not the only, means of creating authentic communities. In a family, one can escape the imperatives of artificial social relationships in favor of belonging to a true community of blood relations in which moral obedience to the authority of another person—the head of the family—is organic and natural. The emphasis that German society places on *Gemütlichkeit*—the coziness of the familiar—is a telling expression of its unusually defensive conception of the private sphere as a place for withdrawal rather than engagement. The private sphere stands in opposition to the external social realm; those outside the family are a priori suspect and not to be trusted, just as the world outside the home is a space of duplicity and inauthenticity.

The particular type of community that the family represented gave rise to two different reactions to the demand for loyalty to the charismatic leader, which the Nazi greeting symbolized, instantiated, and to some extent enforced. One possibility was to reinforce the boundaries of the family sphere and shut oneself off from the outside world and its competing demands. The other possibility was to give in to those demands and, by placing oneself under the total authority of a figure who promised to resolve all conflicts, avoid the burden of responsibility for one's own actions. The nearly 100 percent participation of children and teenagers in the party's youth movements—the Hitler Youth and the League of German Girls—suggests that many young Germans took the Nazi policy of "youth leading youth" as a welcome opportunity to distance themselves from the paternalistic authority of the family by fleeing into the sacralized public realm. The authority of the Führer being far more distant than that of their parents, and the threat of punishment for transgression of that authority much less immediate, the attractions of this choice were hard to resist.[8]

This intergenerational conflict fueled the desire to cede control over one's life to a collectivity and to dilute one's personal responsibility by joining a community of like-minded believers. The ad nauseam repetitions of loyalty declarations that captured the attention of so many foreign observers during the early years of the Third Reich thus come as no surprise. The chairwoman of the National Socialist Women's League, Gertrud Scholtz-Klink, chillingly summed up the ethic of self-surrender: "It is our aim to educate the German girl so that her service to her people will take precedence over everything else. . . . There will be no 'I,' there will be only community."[9] Scholtz-Klink's vision corresponded exactly to the sort of self-image promoted by the regime among its subjects—based on absolute adherence to the collectivity and total rejection of the dignity of individual action. This negation of self permitted Hitler references to penetrate the most basic forms of self-representation, suppressing cognitive and moral dissonance and making it easier for people to blind themselves to what was happening around them.

A common saying during the Third Reich was "If the Führer only knew." The phrase did double duty: it expressed moral disapproval at infractions of any sort by invoking the community's founder, and it transferred to him personally the power to punish. Max Weber described charismatic leadership as being "in brute opposition to all 'patriarchal structures.'"[10] We would be missing the specific nature of Hitler's penetration into the family as well as the specific nature of family relations if we assumed some sort of equivalence between family authority and state power and saw Nazism as merely the continuation of the patriarchal family in the political realm.

Even though, by official decree, Germans were to address Adolf Hitler as "my Führer,"[11] the obligatory possessive pronoun "my" was strangely at odds with the element of distance and mystery in Hitler's persona. But the heightened sense of enigma merely enhanced his charisma, giving rise among ordinary Germans to a compulsion both to overcome the distance and to blame his remoteness on unspecified foreign influences. As Haffner wrote in his *Meaning of Hitler*:

> The Germans preserved a certain awareness of just that [distance] even at the time of their most devout faith in the Führer. Their admiration always had in it a trace of astonishment at the fact that something so unexpected and so strange as Hitler had been vouchsafed them. Hitler to them was a miracle, a "godsend," which, put more prosaically, means someone inexplicably blown in from outside. . . . To the Germans, Hitler has always seemed to come from a long way off—first, for a while, from high heaven; later, may the Lord

have mercy on us, from the deepest abysses of hell.[12]

In the phrase "Heil Hitler," the Führer was a screen onto which private utopias could be projected. At the same time, the oath contained in the greeting reflected people's desire to shed their primary social allegiances.[13] An oath of allegiance creates a bond of blood, a unique relationship, and this sense of one-to-one connection made the Hitler greeting especially appealing to people who experienced the multiplicity of social relations and the gradations of respect and recognition that went along with them as an unbearable burden. Overwhelmed by the demands placed on the self in various areas of life, they could no longer negotiate the boundaries between personal and impersonal relationships. Such people were unable to enlist moral criteria to resist the quasi-religious appeal of an oath of loyalty to an all-powerful secular leader. Singular allegiance to Hitler overshadowed and eventually suppressed the conflicts of competing social demands and relationships that characterize normal society.

Nonetheless, Germans' acceptance of the Hitler greeting in their private lives varied along class lines. Among the lower classes, the Hitler greeting was disproportionately popular because it did away with the rigid formalities of bourgeois social conventions and mores. Psychoanalyst Emma Moersch, who came from a poor background, recalls that in her youth she was uncomfortable with shaking hands because, as a typically bourgeois form of greeting, it reminded her of her relatively low status in society. For her, the Hitler salute represented an innovative practice that promised to end bourgeois custom, replacing it with a direct and unique form of social connection.

Bourgeois circles, of course, reacted differently. The unspoken antiaristocratic sentiment that underlay their social mores had allowed them to cultivate a fragile sense of superiority; they prided themselves on their authenticity and disdained the pretenses of the nobility and the artificiality of its ways. For this reason, they performed the gestures of humility and loyalty demanded of them with a certain distance, with the cynical or desperate courage of those who are used to not ascribing great importance to the situation at hand. In the split second in which they had to make their decision—how to greet, or, if they were greeted first, whether and how to respond—their moral resistance was neutralized by a lapse of perception, a feeling of astonished incredulity or anticipation that they might be corrected. In Walter Kempowski's cycle of autobiographical novels about family life in the Third Reich, the mother, Margarete, often remarks, "We've never seen anything like this," a phrase that expresses indignation after the fact with every bit as much acuity as the question "How can this possibly be?" expresses astonishment at events one sees happening before one's eyes and lets happen. Both attitudes avoid concrete responsibility for reality in much the same way that, on the political level of parties and organizations, bourgeois elites forged their strategies and made their decisions with the anxious certainty and "dignified silence" (Fritz Stern) of those who assure themselves that the worst will soon be over.

The common element in Germans' readiness to accept the new rituals—whether with enthusiasm, indifference, or a sense of scorn—was the hope that the power of Hitler's charisma would free them from the burdens of normal, ambivalent social interactions. This voluntary self-incapacitation led to a general dissolution of moral substance across class and other social lines. Germans lost control of ethical criteria as they ceded moral responsibility for their own actions to a higher, charismatic authority.

The story of the German aristocracy is more complex. The aristocrats were a deeply conservative class, and, because of the prominence of Prussian nobility in the German military, they maintained considerable distance from Nazi etiquette, including the greeting. Immediately after coming to power, Hitler tried to ingratiate himself with the aristocracy by emphasizing the importance of the military—thereby also exploiting aristocratic concepts of soldierly honor to the benefit of the regime. For most of the Nazi period, the nobility, although loyal to the regime, retained considerable autonomy in the private sphere. Representatives of the nobility figured prominently in the anti-Hitler resistance, and late attempts to assassinate the Führer were motivated in part by aristocratic hostility to the Nazi leadership and Nazi mores.

To SUMMARIZE the role played by the greeting in Germany's moral decay: The greeting served to remind Germans of the loyalty they owed their Führer, and it held out an unconditional promise that he would ensure consistency and security in an overly demanding public sphere. It framed a communicative space in which Germans could articulate their aversion to autonomous action and let fate take its course. Finally, the greeting expressed Germans' desire to free themselves from what sociologist Helmuth Plessner characterized as "mediated immediacy" (a term also used to describe Christians' belief in God's indirect presence in every aspect of human lives) in favor of what could be called "nonmediated immediacy," in which the faith in a community embodied by Adolf

Hitler overrode supposedly artificial social customs and moral traditions.

The greeting was a ritual staging of what Nazi ideologues wanted Germans to believe, namely, that National Socialism was an all-encompassing innovation in social customs and the radical break with ordinary daily life that Germans had wished for. As a rite it combined formalism with pathos, self-surrender with moral inexorability. The process by which people accepted the Hitler greeting internally suggests that its offer of charismatic salvation did more than cripple the normal functioning of the public sphere. It also disrupted the minimal requirements of social behavior and warped the relationship between public and private morals by fostering blindness toward the present and a disregard for the fundamental social obligation of respect—for others as well as for oneself. Society was replaced by sacralized community and social obligation by a sense of mission.

It seems possible, therefore, to separate Germans' acceptance of the Hitler greeting from the historical contingency of its appearance at a time of great yearning for belonging and ritual. By doing so, we can begin to understand that acceptance as a process that can occur whenever social obligations, the forms and spaces of communication and participation by which citizens recognize one another, are perceived as too demanding. As the historian Ulrich Herbert observes, "If German society was largely characterized not so much by active, ideologically grounded, fanatical behavior, but rather by indifference, disinterest, and a striking lack of moral values, then genocide does not merely refer to that historically unique situation, that specific German society of the 1930s and 1940s, but becomes oppressively current and urgent, not only, but certainly, here in Germany."[14]

The success of National Socialism cannot be reduced to a

pathological personality type or to some typically German mentality; rather it reflects a will to ignorance, a desire to narrow one's perspective to the point of moral blindness. The inability and unwillingness to recognize the inherent ambivalence and uncertainty of human coexistence continues in radicalisms of various types that seek to rid the social world of its ambiguities—whether through scientific paradigm or through historical determinism. The narrow unilateralism of their perspectives, together with their refusal to respect moral and religious scruples, transcends institutional bounds. Even those fields of activity that enjoy the protection of professional ethics and institutional affiliation are vulnerable, for in the absence of moral questioning, careerist ambitions and material interests tend to flourish unchecked. As Herbert says:

> For judges and those involved in law enforcement, this meant that the idea of eradicating crime by getting rid of criminals could finally become a reality. For some doctors and population scientists, eugenics . . . was finally made official state policy. For the military, the rearmament program signified the long-awaited chance for physical revenge on Germany's former enemies in war. For many entrepreneurs, the destruction of the workers' movement meant the possibility of expanding their businesses without the disruptive influence of workers' rights committees and unions. In short, for numerous groups and professions, Hitler's rise to power opened up opportunities to carry out coveted plans—without any resistance from the people who used to oppose them.[15]

According to Max Weber, "booty obtained through violence or manipulation is one of the typical forms of provision for needs" by which charismatic authority assures itself of popular approbation.[16] In Germany, the looting began within the nation itself, then extended beyond its borders, setting off a world war. Once a community that regards itself as a morally privileged elect sees its mission as succeeding, then looting becomes possible in a metaphorical sense as well: in the aforementioned professions, the confiscated booty was doubt and protest.

CHAPTER SEVEN

The Long Shadow of
a Fatal Gesture

IN 1946, DIPLOMAT WILHELM MELCHERS RECALLED A meeting he had in 1944 with his colleague Adam von Trott, at which Trott informed him of a plot to assassinate Hitler—the famous ill-fated plot of July 20. "I took Trott's hand," Melchers remembered, "and said, 'I can't believe that this horrible pressure is really going to be lifted from us. July 20th is a date we'll never forget.' For a while we were silent. Then Trott pointed to his desk. On it was a letter that ended with the obligatory 'Heil Hitler.' Suddenly Trott laughed and whispered, 'Now I'll no longer have to sign letters with this wretched greeting.'"[1]

With the end of the war and the collapse of Hitler's dictatorship, the German greeting fell into almost complete disuse. One reads scattered anecdotes about individuals for whom stretching out their right arms had become second nature and who had difficulty bringing their habits into line with the new realities. German POWs in Allied war camps continued to use the salute, it seems. Norbert Steinhauser, a museum director in the town of Friedrichshafen, recalled an arrangement between his parents on their Sunday walks, whereby his mother always took his father's right hand to prevent him from reflexively saluting. As a university student at Tübingen in 1946, Irving Fetscher attended a lecture by philosopher Ludwig Klages, who began his talk by intoning the words "an ancient gesture of blessing" as he slowly stretched forth his right arm. I myself have come across a cache of letters from September 1945, in which the author signs off with the phrase "with friendly German greetings"—an isolated instance apparently, a hybrid form on the road back to the bourgeois formula "with friendly greetings" which is still in current use.

Today, the Hitler greeting is practiced only among a tiny subculture of the socially disaffected and economically vulnerable, who can count on the sheer scandal value of this publicly reviled gesture to garner media attention. While such forms of the greeting's afterlife rely on provocation to penetrate the public space, the greeting persists in silent, more covert ways as well, for example, on customized license plates with the letters "HH" in the middle or the number 88—H being the eighth letter of the alphabet. This particular usage crossed the German border some years ago and functions as a not-so-secret sign of recognition among self-styled conspiracy cultists and members of racist counterculture groups. The double-8 has even penetrated the world of fashion and shows up now and then on mass-market silk-screened T-shirts, which are often bought and sometimes even designed by people unaware of its dark provenance.

This need for camouflage is a consequence of the fact that the Nazi salute is not only reviled but also illegal. Section 86 of the German Penal Code provides for punishment of up to three years in prison and fines for anyone using symbols "associated with unconstitutional organizations"—symbols being defined to include "flags, badges, uniforms, slogans, and forms of greeting." The law explicitly bans the phrases "Heil Hitler" or "With German greetings" in written correspondence as well as the use of Sieg Heil in public speech. The sole exceptions are usages that are "ironic and clearly critical of the Hitler greeting," and this exemption has led to scattered legal debates as to what constitutes an ironic use of the salute. One recent case involved Prince Albrecht of Hannover, who was brought to court after using the gesture as a tacit commentary on the behavior of an overly zealous airport baggage inspector.

It is easy to lose sight of the pervasiveness of the Hitler salute. During the Third Reich, the Hitler greeting was performed billions of times, at the beginning of an encounter and at the end; it was spoken enthusiastically, perfunctorily, or hesitantly, in barely audible whispers and in loud choruses. There is much we still do not know about its use, especially in the small passing moments of daily life. Did people begin with "Heil Hitler" when they asked for directions on the street, for example? What happened at the doctor's office, in this ephemeral site of a communicative community—two people united temporarily through illness, in other words, strangers to each other yet intimate at the same time? How did neighbors initiate a conversation across a garden fence when planting spring bulbs or harvesting the last tomatoes in early fall? Can it really be that Germans in their private lives took leave of one another, as the edicts demanded, with "Heil Hitler" instead of a congenial "Auf Wiedersehen"? It is possible that we will never have answers to questions like these, but what is certain is that, as the emblematic gesture of a dark and barbaric time, the Hitler salute has cast a long shadow, both within Germany and abroad, upon public demonstrations of German national pride. Every time a German politician raises an arm to return the affection of a crowd of supporters, he risks awakening memories of the stiff-armed salute. An unwritten protocol forbids excessively self-celebratory expressions of national feeling in favor of measure and restraint. For example, at the Munich Olympic Games in 1972, the event that more than any other signaled the Federal Republic's postwar rehabilitation, the behavior of the German team throughout the proceedings—from the way they entered the stadium, greeting the crowd with smiling faces and casual, friendly waves, to their relaxed posture on the victors' podiums—was designed to present a counterimage to the rigid ceremonialism of the National Socialist period. Even now, more than fifty years after the end of the Third Reich, debates continue over the proper contours and expressions of German patriotism. In this sense, too, the ritualized pathos of the Nazi regime continues to affect German society, if only in the quest to break with it.

OUR INVESTIGATION of the Hitler salute has tried to show how it ceased to be a mere gesture of group membership and, by becoming a perpetual homage to the Führer, changed the basic foundations of communication. It usurped the role of normal greetings and in doing so deformed their purpose. At the heart of our study has been the question of "how": How could people trade a customary communicative practice for a new one; how did the new practice become routine and establish itself as a tradition in its own right; how did a form of social behavior that had no precedent in Germany entrench itself in daily life and become second nature? The answer to many of these questions, as we have tried to show, lies in the fact that the Hitler greeting was not a greeting at all, appearances notwithstanding. The process by which the Nazi salute could assume the aspects of something it was not was described by Max Weber, whose terminology we have borrowed throughout this study. Weber wrote:

> When the tide that lifted a charismatically led group out of everyday life flows back into the channels of workaday routines, at least the "pure" form of charismatic domination will wane and turn into an "institution"; it is then either mechanized, as it were, or imperceptibly displaced by other structures, or fused with them in the most diverse forms, so that it becomes a mere component of a concrete historical structure. In this case it is often transformed beyond recognition, and identifiable only on an analytical level.[2]

In just this way, the Hitler salute fused with the structural principles of the greeting, turned it into a loyalty oath and membership badge, and thus utterly distorted its normal function as a gesture of mutual acknowledgment and reciprocal commitment.

PEOPLE ACCEPTED the new greeting for various reasons. The desperate fanatics who embraced it as a way of avoiding the trials and burdens of human encounters and social exchange set the tone for the apathetic ones, who felt themselves superior to their own actions and conformed to the new edicts as though their acts were not their own. The former celebrated the new rituals as a welcome substitute for law and social convention, while the latter fooled themselves into thinking the new rituals were a passing phenomenon, even as they helped make them established practice. Self-disempowerment went hand in hand with self-stupefaction.

For those in power and their supporters, to perform the Hitler greeting was to display their alignment with the Nazi ideals, but it would be too simple to read the gesture as a sign of unambiguous support. For, as we have seen, people also saluted opportunistically, defensively, or even to express resistance, albeit veiled and modest. Nevertheless, whatever the specific context of its use or the intention of the individual using it, the content itself—that Germans should be ever ready to sacrifice their own interests and values for the regime, and that their everyday, real-life behavior was part of a sacred, trans-historical mission—was an error and a lie. And in getting people to speak this lie, the Hitler salute turned the very idea of human communication on its head, as Samuel Beckett seems to have understood. The three exclamation points with which he ended his observation about what he saw above the portal to the Dominican church can be read in hindsight as a call, a way of drawing our attention to the inversion of meaning that the Hitler greeting represented and to the destructive energy that it heralded and helped to unleash.

GREETINGS ARE a microcosmic embodiment of social relations, and what this study of greetings suggests is that it may be possible to gain insight into the moral perversions of National Socialism without recourse to the stereotype of a supposedly German national character—inherently anti-Semitic, predisposed to authoritarianism, and afflicted with a sense of being history's victims. Instead, we might look at the breakdown in people's sense of self that allowed them to disassociate present actions from future consequences and fostered indifference to those present before them. These two phenomena—erosion of a sense of self and moral disregard—together formed a vicious circle that impeded Germans' interactions with one another and encouraged them to prefer a ritual to actual human contact. The story of the Hitler greeting is a tale of how Germans tried to evade the responsibility of normal social intercourse, rejected the gift of contact with others, allowed social mores to decay, and refused to acknowledge the inherent openness and ambivalence of human relationships and social exchange.

Theodor W. Adorno once remarked that Hitler had confiscated laughter. In the same vein we might say that the Hitler salute confiscated the act of greeting, and with it the possibility of expressing one of the fundamental forms of human sociability. Germans may have thought that by regressing to the rites of premodernity they could rid themselves of the burdens and ambivalences that are part of social exchange, but in their embrace of the Hitler salute, they gave up something else as well: the natural ease of human encounters, one of the legacies of civilization.

Moral reflection does not like to concern itself with small things; it prefers grand gestures. Greetings, however, present us with an exception to this rule, for they are an integral part of our sociability. They remind us of the need to live our lives by linking them to those of our fellow human beings. They make us aware of the connection between anticipation and memory, the future and the past, and of our own relationship to both. Greetings are the most "sacred" aspect of sociability and our relations with one another; to greet someone is to offer the most precious of gifts: presence and approachability. Greetings reassure us of our existence here and now, for ourselves and for others. The intrinsic reciprocity of the greeting exchange, the give and take of saying "hello" and "good-bye," contains a moral recognition of our dependence on one another.

We are still living with the history of the fatal gesture that was the Hitler salute, and one of the lessons of that history is that we need to be wary of obligatory rituals, especially when they are imposed from above. Nevertheless, with regard to the greeting, there is one obligation we should embrace, which is to respect and pay tribute to its value, while keeping in mind the dark memory of its perversion.

Notes

CHAPTER ONE: SHAPING THE BEGINNING

1. José Ortega y Gasset, "Reflections on the Salutation. Etymological Man. What Is a Usage?" *Man and People* (New York: W. W. Norton & Company, 1957), 207–8.
2. I thank Fritz Weigle for this reference.
3. Albert Schoop, *Als der Krieg zu Ende ging* (Frauenfeld: Huber, 1985), 34.

CHAPTER TWO: THE GREETING AS INITIAL GIFT

1. My sketch refers to a number of works from various academic disciplines. The discussion of the greeting as communicative practice is based on works of ethnology, linguistics, and speech act theory (Schegloff, Searles) as well as micro-sociology (Erving Goffman, *Relations in Public: Microstudies of the Public Order* [New York: Basic Books, 1971]). The idea of the greeting as "space for sociality," offering the possibility of social exchange and human individuation, comes from structuralism, in particular from the works of Marcel Mauss. Mauss's ideas have been further developed by the German sociologist Ulrich Oevermann.
2. One of the earliest sociological studies of the greeting, *Theorie der Sitte* ("Theory of Mores"), by the German legal historian Rudolf von Jhering, published in 1886, already offered a modern approach to the greeting's

dual function of establishing sociality and delineating its historically limited form. Jhering writes of an "ethics of social intercourse": "What interest does society have in social intercourse? With this question, we hit upon a fundamental point . . . which holds the key to our understanding of this aspect of our lives. Social intercourse is a social institution and a social duty." *Der Zweck im Recht,* vol. 2 (Leipzig: Breitkopf & Härtel, 1886), 339.

3. Gestures of greeting, particularly the use of the head and hands, emphasize, differentiate, and comment on the message communicated by the greeting's verbal element. Rudolf von Jhering (*Der Zweck im Recht,* vol. 2 [Leipzig: Breitkopf & Härtel, 1886], 652) writes: "The fact that two people perceive themselves to be unified or connected is made most evident by the physical representation of their union. The stages of this symbolic unity proceed from the hands (shaking hands) to the arms (embracing) to the lips (kissing)." On the role of the hand in establishing "direct social contact," see also Heinrich Popitz, *Der Aufbruch zur artifiziellen Gesellschaft. Zur Anthropologie der Technik* (Tübingen: Mohr Siebeck, 1995), 61.

4. To follow Gennep's line of analysis, spatial passages and crossings are what necessitate the ritualization of human communication and the greeting in particular: "The various forms of greeting belong to the category of membership rites. They vary according to how foreign a new arrival is to the residents of a house or community. The diverse forms of greetings used among Christians, which have been preserved in their archaic forms in the Slavic countries—as well as the Muslim *salaam*—constantly renew the mystical bond of membership in the same religion." Arnold van Gennep, *Übergangsriten* (Frankfurt: Campus, 1999), 40.

5. Ulrich Oevermann, "Die Methode der Fallrekonstruktion in der Grundlagenforschung sowie der klinischen und padagogischen Praxis," in K. Kraimer, ed., *Die Fallrekonstruktion. Sinnverstehen in der sozialwissenschaftlichen Forschung* (Frankfurt: Suhrkamp, 2000), 136.

6. See Raymond Firth in J. S. La Fontaine, ed., *The Interpretation of Ritual* (London: Routledge, 2004), 32.

CHAPTER FOUR: AN OATH BY ANY OTHER NAME

1. *Der Völkische Beobachter,* 79, March 1935. Cited in Wolfgang Kratzer, *Feiern und Feste der Nationalsozialisten: Aneignung und Umgestaltung*

christlicher Kalender, Riten und Symbole (University dissertation, 1998), 116.

2. Private interview with former German President Johannes Rau.

3. Rudolf Schmidt, *Der praktische Schulmann* (Frankfurt: Friedrich Brandstetter, 1936), 98.

4. Matthias Wegner, *Ein weites Herz. Die zwei Leben der Isa Vermehren* (Munich: Claassen Verlag, 2003), 38.

5. Ingeborg Schäfer and Susanne Klockmann, *Mutter mochte Himmler nie. Die Geschichte einer SS-Familie* (Reinbek: Rowohlt, 1999), 57.

6. Tomi Unger, *Die Gedanken sind frei. Meine Kindheit im Elsaß* (Zürich: Diogenes Verlag, 2000), 92.

7. Bertl Valentin, *Du bleibst ja da und zwar sofort! Mein Vater Karl Valentin* (Munich: Piper Verlag GmbH, 1982), 150.

8. Samuel Beckett, "Alles kommt auf soviel an," *German Diaries* (Hamburg: Hoffmann und Campe, 2003), 15.

9. E. Grohne, "Gruß und Gebärden," *Handbuch der deutschen Volkskunde*, vol. 1 (Leipzig: Gysbers & Van Loon, 1934–1935), 315–24. The language used in the contemporary issue of the *Brockhaus* encyclopedia is similar.

10. Martha Dodd, *Through Embassy Eyes* (New York: Harcourt, Brace and Company, 1939), 244–45.

11. The rules in one high school in the town of Colmar read: "There are to be no other forms of greeting before the German greeting."

12. See Wolfgang Neuber in Hans Wienicke, ed., *Schon damals fingen viele an zu schweigen . . .: Quellensammlung zur Geschichte Charlottenburgs von 1933–1945* (National Archives), 32.

CHAPTER FIVE: THE RISE OF THE SPHERE OF MISTRUST

1. See Brigitte Hamann, *Hitler's Vienna: A Dictator's Apprenticeship* (New York: Oxford University Press, 1999), 236.

2. See Simonetta Falasca-Zamponi's excellent study *Fascist Spectacle: The Aesthetics of Power in Mussolini's Italy* (Berkeley: University of California Press, 1997).

3. Benito Mussolini, *Scritti e discorsi di Benito Mussolini*, vol. 2 (Milan: U. Hoepli, 1934–1939), 163.

4. A report about a train journey through Schleswig-Holstein described that Northern German region as "thoroughly National Socialist. People

getting on and off the train only used 'Heil Hitler' " (Werner Jochmann, *Nationalsozialismus und Revolution. Ursprung und Geschichte der NSDAP in Hamburg 1922–1933* [Frankfurt: Europäische, 1963], 418–19). See also Martin Broszat and Elke Fröhlich, *Bayern in der NS-Zeit*, 6 vols. (Munich and Vienna: Oldenbourg, 1979–1983).

5. See Hans Wienicke, ed., *Schon damals fingen viele an zu schweigen . . .*, 123.

6. The monkeys' owners were also subject to punishment. Traubert Petter—a traveling vaudeville performer who was known for his powerful voice and who worked with monkeys—was sent to the Eastern Front in 1940, and an order was issued for his animals to be destroyed, after he was found to have violated the antidefamation ordinance. Miraculously, both he and his monkeys survived.

7. See Claude R. Foster, *Paul Schneider* (West Chester, Penn.: West Chester University, 1995).

8. Viktor Klemperer, *I Shall Bear Witness: The Diaries of Viktor Klemperer, 1933–41* (London: Weidenfeld & Nicolson, 1998), 67.

9. Erhard Eppler, *Als Wahrheit verordnet wurde* (Frankfurt: Insel, 1994), 62.

10. Viktor Klemperer, *I Shall Bear Witness*, 68.

11. Thomas Wolfe, *You Can't Go Home Again* (New York: Harper & Brothers, 1940), 618.

12. Karl Löwith, *Mein Leben in Deutschland vor und nach 1993* (Stuttgart: J. B. Metzler, 1986), 129.

13. Walter Kempowski, *Tadellöser und Wolff* (Munich: Carl Hanser Verlag, 1971), 198.

CHAPTER SIX: DEVALUING THE PRESENT

1. Max Weber, *Economy and Society: An Outline of Interpretive Sociology* (Berkeley: University of California Press, 1978), 245.

2. On February 28, 1933, four weeks after Hitler was appointed German chancellor, the government issued an emergency decree for the "Protection of the People and State," suspending normal civil liberties. Three weeks later, the Reichstag approved the Enabling Act, which gave the executive branch of the government legislative authority. The principle of separation of powers was completely abandoned, and Germany effectively became a one-party state. With the death of Hindenburg on Au-

gust 2, 1934, the offices of Reich president and Reich chancellor were merged, and the Führer principle, according to which Hitler could make dictatorial decisions, was institutionally established.

3. Klaus Scholder, *Die Kirchen und das Dritte Reich, Bd. 1: Vorgeschichte und Zeit der Illusionen, 1918–1934* (Berlin: Propyläen, 1977).

4. Karl Barth and Emil Brunner, *Letters 1916–1966*, in Karl Barth, *Gesamtausgabe*, vol. 5: *Briefe* (Zurich: Theologischer Verlag, 2000), 275.

5. See Eric Voegelin, *Die politischen Religionen* (Munich: Fink, 1996) and Ernst Troeltsch, *Die Soziallehren der christlichen Kirchen und Gruppen* (Aalen: Scientia Verlag, 1921).

6. Rudolf Absolon, *Die Wehrmacht im Dritten Reich*, vol. 6 (Freiburg: Oldenbourg, 1993), 204.

7. Sebastian Haffner, *Defying Hitler* (New York: Farrar, Straus and Giroux, 2002), 185.

8. I thank Rolf Haubl for this observation.

9. Interview in the *Deutsche Allgemeine Zeitung*, September 16, 1934.

10. Max Weber, *Economy and Society*, 244.

11. In a letter to the Reich's foreign minister Joachim von Ribbentrop, Hans-Heinrich Lammers, the head of the Reich Chancellery, laid out requirements for non-Germans. Because the word "Führer" could not be adequately translated into other languages, Lammers reported, "the Führer has decided that 'the Führer of the Greater German Empire' is the form of address that best expresses his own dignified position and that of the German Empire he represents. It should be used in all official communications with foreign countries. . . . As an oral form of address, Germans are to say 'my Führer' . . . foreigners should simply use the word 'Führer.' I hereby empower you to inform all foreigners who want to be received by the Führer as to this matter of protocol." Beatrice Heiber and Helmut Heiber, eds., *Die Rückseite des Hakenkreuzes. Absonderliches aus den Akten des Dritten Reiches* (Munich: dtv-Dokumente, 1993), 95.

12. Sebastian Haffner, *The Meaning of Hitler* (London: Weidenfeld and Nicolson, 1979), 164.

13. Psychologist Tilmann Moser cites a German woman of the postwar period interrogating her mother about her admiration for Hitler. The daughter's questions are telling: "How you must have hated yourself to fall so in love with Hitler! Is there a connection? Did he make you like yourself or at

least put an end to your self-hatred and envy?" Tilmann Moser, *Dämonische Figuren. Die Wiederkehr des Dritten Reiches in der Psychotherapie* (Frankfurt: Suhrkamp, 1999), 115.

14. Ulrich Herbert, *National Socialist Extermination Policies: Contemporary German Perspectives and Controversies* (Oxford: Berghan Books, 1999), 43.

15. Ulrich Herbert, ed., *Nationalsozialistische Vernichtungspolitik 1939–1945. Neue Forschungen und Kontroversen* (Frankfurt: Fischer, 1998), 35.

16. Max Weber, *Economy and Society*, 245.

CHAPTER SEVEN: THE LONG SHADOW OF A FATAL GESTURE

1. Citied in Wilhelm Haas, *Beitrag zur Geschichte der Entstehung des Auswärtigen Dienstes der Bundesrepublik Deutschland* (Bremen: Selbstverlag, 1969), 400.

2. Max Weber, *Economy and Society*, vol. 3, Guenther Roth and Claus Wittich, eds. (New York: Bedminster Press, 1968), 1121.

Acknowledgments

In writing this book, I relied first of all on numerous conversations with people who lived through the time of the obligatory Hitler salute. My thanks to all who contributed their private experiences to this work of reconstruction. I would also like to thank the following people for their help and encouragement in the preparation of the manuscript: Christa Allert, Karin Eichhoff-Cyrus, Rolf Haubl, Lorenz Jäger, Reinhard Pabst, Jochen Schäfers, and Adolf Vees. My special gratitude goes to Rainer M. Lepsius. Discussions with him accompanied every stage of my work on this book, and his own analysis of National Socialism was the inspiration behind my attempt to decipher Germans' inner acceptance of a charismatic promise.

Illustration Credits

Page 57: Hitler and Mussolini near Salzburg, April 22, 1944, © Ullstein Bilderdienst

Page 60: Traubert Petter and chimpanzee, 1935, used with the kind permission of the Petter family

Page 62: From Heinrich Schulz, "Mühlenfibel," ca. 1934

Page 64: From "Jung Deutschland-Fibel," Paul Hartung, Hamburg, 1940

Page 77: Abbot Alban Schachleiter, Upper Bavaria, July 1, 1934 © Ullstein Bilderdienst

Index

Page numbers in italics refer to illustrations.

ABOUT THE AUTHOR

TILMAN ALLERT was born in 1947 and is currently professor of sociology at the Johann Wolfgang Goethe University of Frankfurt. His research specialties are micro-sociology and the sociology of the family. His book *The Family: Case Studies in the Indestructibility of a Form of Life,* which appeared in 1999, won him the Christa Hoffmann-Riem Prize for Qualitative Social Research.

ABOUT THE TRANSLATOR

JEFFERSON CHASE'S translations include the Signet edition of Thomas Mann's *Death in Venice and Other Stories, Hitler's Beneficiaries* by Götz Aly, and *The Culture of Defeat* by Wolfgang Schivelbusch. He lives in Berlin.